ON BECOMING
A CATHOLIC

The Challenge of
Christian Initiation

Regis A. Duffy, O.F.M.

1817

Harper & Row, Publishers, San Francisco

Cambridge, Hagerstown, New York, Philadelphia
London, Mexico City, São Paulo, Singapore, Sydney

For my fellow friars,
Vincent, Joseph, Kenneth, and William,
with whom I share a common vision and a future hope

FIRST EDITION

Library of Congress Cataloging in Publication Data

Duffy, Regis A.
   ON BECOMING A CATHOLIC.

   Includes index.
   1. Initiation rites—Catholic Church. 2. Catholic Church—
Doctrines. I. Title.
BX1968.D84   1984   265   84-47721
ISBN 0-06-062107-9 (pbk.)

85 86 87 88 10 9 8 7 6 5 4 3 2

CONTENTS

ACKNOWLEDGMENTS

Without the assistance and encouragement of others, theological research and writing might prove impossible tasks. My own work continues to benefit from the informed interest of others, and I gladly acknowledge it.

I wish to thank Dr. B. Marthaler, O.F.M. Conv., for his gracious invitation to deliver the first Mary Charles Bryce, O.S.B., lecture at the Catholic University of America. I have incorporated major sections of the research for that lecture into Chapter 2. I should also like to express my gratitude to Dr. R. Duggan, who invited me to contribute an article, ''The Rights and Rituals of Commitment,'' to the book *Conversion and the Catechumenate* (New York: Paulist, 1984). Some of the material from that article appears throughout this book and is used with permission.

Finally, I wish to thank my editor, John Loudon of Harper & Row, Publishers, who initiated this project (once again) and contributed to its conclusion by his enthusiastic and perceptive assistance.

REGIS A. DUFFY, O.F.M.

The Washington Theological Union
Easter Monday, April 23, 1984

INTRODUCTION

When the Trappist monk Thomas Merton published his autobiographical *The Seven Storey Mountain* in 1948, the book created a stir similar to that of Augustine's *Confessions* (ca. 387), if we are to judge by contemporary accounts.[1] Merton reviews his problem of becoming fully Christian after his conversion, a brief period of instructions, and then his baptism and first eucharist: "Six weeks of instruction, after all, were not much, and I certainly had nothing but the barest rudiments of knowledge about the actual practice of Catholic life, *and if I had not made the absolutely tragic assumption that now my period of training was finished and done with, I would not have made such a mess of that first year after my Baptism.*"[2]

Yet there is one important difference between the adult conversion and initiation of Thomas Merton and Augustine of Hippo that is often overlooked. Augustine, enrolled as a catechumen since a youth, received his Christian formation within the catechumenate of St. Ambrose, bishop of Milan, who had himself been in a similar catechumenal situation as a young man. The catechumenate was an initiation process of formation that was integrated into the larger life of the Christian community. Ideally this process touched every dimension of the catechumen's life—affective, moral, intellectual, and social. Nor did the catechumenal process end with the Easter Vigil's celebration of the sacraments of initiation. The mystagogical or post-Easter insertion into the life and mission of the community was considered a source of renewal for the whole community. Augustine speaks from personal experience when he gives his famous axiom: "For it is the church that gives birth to all."[3]

If Thomas Merton were being initiated into the Church today, he would participate in a very different experience. In 1972, the Roman Catholic Church restored the catechumenal process of Christian initiation for adults that Ambrose, Augustine, and so many other Christians had profited from in the early centuries. (The official text for this process is called "Rite of Christian Initiation of Adults," but will be referred to throughout this book by the abbreviation that is in common use—RCIA.[4]) The process is divided into four continuous stages that correspond to the candidate's progress in Christian formation: a precatechumenal period of initiation conversion and inquiry; a catechumenal period of affective, moral, intellectual, and ecclesial formation; a period of final preparation for the sacraments of initiation; and the postbaptismal period of ongoing insertion into the life and mission of the Christian community.[5]

The catechumenal process is not, however, an updated form of "religious instructions" of the kind Merton received in the thirties. The sacraments of initiation are the model for the whole sacramental life of the Church. Unlike the baptism of infants, who cannot request initiation, adults must freely seek to be Christian, to commit themselves to the gospel values and perspectives on every level of their lives, and to redirect their energies to the building of the Kingdom of God. Just as the Christian cannot receive another sacrament without having first been initiated into the Church, so the sacraments of initiation set the criteria for the honest participation of those Christians already initiated.

The RCIA, then, is directed, first of all, to those who consider themselves to be Christian. But is less to be required of us to become more fully Christian than of those who are candidates? Second, the RCIA addresses the local church. What happens if we, in effect, are preparing catechumens for a local church that remains unchallenged by the very demands made on the unbaptized or those returning to the practice of their faith? The RCIA does not assume a perfect Christian community, but it does challenge us, as Paul did the Thessalonians, to "comfort and upbuild one another, as indeed you are doing. . . . Do not stifle the Spirit" (1 Thess. 5:11,19).[6] The RCIA is an accurate test, then, of the actual praxis of the local Christian community or parish—of its real priorities, values, and sense of mission. This process suggests some penetrating questions about what the local church expects of those she invites to receive, for example, the sacraments of confirmation and marriage.

Third, the catechumenal process affords those who were baptized as infants but who have never, as adults, appropriated or invested themselves in that faith the opportunity to reassess their life experience and God's part in it. The RCIA is an integrated experience that enables disaffected, disenchanted, or bored Christians to reexamine their situation from a very different, and perhaps surprising, perspective.

Finally, the RCIA is the embodied welcome of the Church to all who wish to know Christ and be part of his work of building a peaceable kingdom. Thomas Merton ultimately found his continuing formation as a Christian within a core Christian community of Trappist monks. But every would-be Christian must learn "to be as Christ" within the experience of a community of Christians. Large, anonymous gatherings of Christians do not suffice for the formation of catechumens or, for that matter, of the baptized.

The RCIA forcefully reminds us that initiation is a challenge. "Challenge" connotes the effort required to become and remain Christian. (The word "challenge" originally meant that someone could keep a prize until another could win it away.) Initiation challenges both the Christian community, its individual members, and uninitiated but interested candidates. This shared challenge is rooted in the mission of the Christian community. To be Christian, in a word, is to have an experience of God's future Kingdom in the flawed Church community of the present. Augustine thought of such groups as "begetting communities" in which all shared in the process of becoming and remaining Christian.

The six chapters of this book attempt to articulate some of the challenges implicit in the catechumenal process. The careful reader will note that the sequence of chapters follows the stages of the catechumenate. Chapter 1 takes up the questions of evangelization, the precatechumenal period. Chapters 2 through 4 reflect the challenges of the catechumenal stage. Chapter 5 discusses some of the theological implications of the period of the enlightenment and of Easter initiation. The final chapter takes up some of the larger questions of the mystagogical or postinitiation period.

The first chapter deals with the theology of the Cross as the root of all Christian conversion and formation. The first challenge is addressed to the whole Christian community: Is there a conflict between our theologies of the Cross and the actual praxis of our Christian parishes or individual lives? There is always the danger of making the mystery of salvation and its expression in a crucified Lord more "manageable" by reducing it to theological statements or ritual signs of the Cross. Yet the theology of the Cross shapes the self-awareness of the Church always—in the process of conversion, its sense of mission, morality, witness, and the sacred. Just as Paul learns the meaning of the Cross through his encounter with the risen Lord, so the Church is constantly brought back to that event by the same Lord in its midst. The catechumenal process follows the Pauline route of rediscovering the meaning of the Cross for our shared lives.

The second chapter uncovers another challenge of initiation; the radical way in which God's Word transforms our words: Does the Word of God continue to be a prophetic Word in our parishes, and in our familial and personal lives? Catechumens, like the baptized, must learn to sit and eat at the table of God's Word. Like the disciples on their way to Emmaus, we need the Word of God to understand his vision and to clarify our intentions. For the Word of God is an experience of the presence of God that uncovers the praxis of our own lives. But the proclamation of the Word of God is much more than reading scriptural selections *at* Christians assembled for the eucharist. It is more than enduring homelies that seem sometimes to be devoid of content or relevancy. God's Word calls us, as it did the Emmaus disciples, to "recognize" the Lord in the unexpected places of our lives and our world. The second chapter, then, deals not only with precatechumenal evangelization, but with the ongoing listening and response to the Word of God that characterizes the lives of both catechumens and the baptized.

Chapter 3 offers another challenge of initiation: Are our intentions honorable? To be Christian is to "walk" a certain way, that is, to live and act in the distinct manner of someone marked by the Cross and the Word of God. The catechumenal process is one of conversion that profoundly questions our priorities, values, and lifestyle. Just as a lens focuses the reality which we look at, so our intentions are our way of "seeing" or making sense out of our experience and world. Learning to be Christian always involves Christ's meaning and values challenging our own. In one way or another, the symbolic actions of worship and sacrament, which are filled with the presence of God, must reflect our own intentions to accept and share in his meanings. To express it differently, there is nothing more deceptive than a sacrament in which Christ's meanings do not challenge our own.

The fourth chapter draws out some of the corollaries implicit in the catechumenal process. First, the Christian community must continue to pose the question: What should we ask of catechumens? In answering that question, she also sketches out the profile of what it means to be a Christian community. But within such a community, how are teachers called out who know how to educate both catechumens and Christians alike to love a mystery? The sacraments of initiation, after all, celebrate the paschal mystery, the presence of a crucified and risen Lord in our midst. Good teacher that she is, the Church leads us into the experience of a renewed sense of sacred time, the liturgical year, in which the rich complexity of the paschal mystery is symbolized. On the other hand, why does the liturgical year seem to be irrelevant to so many Christians? Does the Christian, in fact, have a different sense of time than his or her "secular" counterpart?

How do we enable one another to serve again, and thus, honor our initiation commitment? This challenge opens up the discussion of the fifth chapter which deals with the final period of preparation for the reception of the sacraments of initiation—Lent. The Lenten observance originated historically in the clash of imperfect commitments within the Christian community. As the catechumens entered a final period of scrutiny and penance, the need of the baptized for continuing conversion was underlined all the more sharply. Behind the dramatic catechumenal celebrations of Lent, such as exorcism and the "handing over" of the Creed and the Our Father, there is a practical theology of our redemptive need and God's enduring response. To grasp the meaning of Good Friday and Easter, we can do no better than entering the catechumenal context of these celebrations. To be baptized into the death and resurrection of Christ and to be anointed with the Spirit is to experience the Easter event.

The final chapter, "The Easter Mondays of the Christian Life," leads us back to the situation of Thomas Merton after his baptism. The post-Easter challenge of initiation can be summed up in the question: Where do we go with the experience of resurrection? The success of the postinitiation period hinges on the continuing insertion of the neophytes into the Christian community. We examine the implications of Easter for the Church through the last of the initiation sacraments, the eucharist. The sacrament of the eucharist is, after all, participation in the death of the Lord. But what are the implications of such participation for the Christian community as well as the individual? Eucharistic participation is the way in which we flesh out the commitments of initiation. Honest participation in the eucharist is tested by a renewed sense of mission and ministry in the community, and a personal willingness to die daily, to use Paul's evocative phrase (2 Cor. 4:10–12).

There are already a number of helpful books which deal with the various pastoral, theological, and historical dimensions of the catechumente.[7] This book, however, continues to explore the question raised in my earlier writings: What is the relation between what we do (praxis) and what we teach (theory)?[8] The catechumenate, I would submit, represents a praxis of initiation that helps clarify the theology of redemption, Church, and sacrament. Theologians and those engaged in pastoral ministry can benefit from a closer examination of the implications of the RCIA for their work. Those engaged in the various teachings ministries of the Church can profit from one of the most successful pedagogical models the Church has ever used. Those responsible for formation in religious life could find no better guide for helping candidates than that of Christian discipleship sketched in the RCIA. Above all, the catechumenate was, and can be again, the normal way in which the parish community renews and reforms itself.

NOTES

1. P. Brown, *Augustine of Hippo* (Berkeley: University of California, 1969), pp. 177–81.
2. Thomas Merton, *The Seven Storey Mountain* (New York: Harcourt, Brace, 1948), p. 228 (my emphasis).
3. Augustine, *On Baptism*, I, 15, in *Nicene and Post-Nicene Fathers* IV (Grand Rapids: W. B. Eerdmans, 1979), p. 421.
4. The English translation of the RCIA may be found in *The Rites of the Catholic Church* (New York: Pueblo, 1976), pp. 13–81. For some of the background of the *Ordo* of initiation and its theological development during preliminary drafts, see R. Duggan, "Conversion in the '*Ordo Initiationis Christianae Adultorum*'," *Ephemerides Liturgicae* 96(1982):57–83.
5. Initiation includes the sacraments of baptism, confirmation, and eucharist.
6. I employ the New American Bible translation of scriptural passages unless otherwise noted. Underlined passages in scriptural passages are obviously my emphases.
7. To cite but a few, *Made, Not Born: New Perspectives on Christian Initiation and the Catechumenate* (Notre Dame: University of Notre Dame, 1976); *Becoming a Catholic Christian* (New York: Sadlier, 1978); M. Dujarier, *A History of the Catechumenate* (New York: Sadlier, 1979); idem, *The Rites of Christian Initiation* (New York: Sadlier, 1979); A. Kavanagh, *The Shape of Baptism: The Rite of Christian Initiation* (New York: Pueblo, 1978); the periodical, *Resources of Christian Initiation* (published by quarterly by Sadlier); R. Duggan, ed., *Conversion and the Catechumenate* (New York: Paulist, 1984).
8. *Real Presence: Worship, Sacraments, and Commitment* (San Francisco: Harper & Row, 1982; idem, *A Roman Catholic Theology of Pastoral Care* (Philadelphia: Fortress, 1983).

Chapter 1

STONE OF STUMBLING?

One of the stranger questions of the New Testament is found in Paul's first letter to the Corinthians: "Was it Paul who was crucified for you?" (1 Cor. 1:13). Although the question may sound rhetorical, Christian communities do not always act as if they know the answer. This is the context, in fact, of Paul's question, for this Christian community at Corinth seems to have lost its sense of direction. One practical indication of this problem, then and now, is the way in which the message of the Cross and its consequences have been muted in the shared living of the community.

Paul's question is still the proper starting point for any book that deals with the process of becoming Christian. That process of initiation is always rooted in a community that has been shaped by the meaning of Christ's death. If Paul sometimes speaks of Christ's death for us without mentioning his resurrection, it is not because the latter teaching is less important. But Paul has learned that Christian communities tend to pass over too quickly the implication of the Cross for their lives so that they can relax in the security of their own theologies of resurrection.

This chapter takes up Paul's question once again by asking if there is a conflict between our theologies of the Cross and the ways in which we live out our understanding of initiation in our parishes, religious communities, families, and personal experiences. Suppose a Christian community has a crucifix on the walls of its church but does not deal with the radical implications of the Cross? Suppose a parish has sophisticated programs of religious instruction and preaching that incorporate a theory about the Cross, but one is hard put to find it being lived out within that community? In such communities, Paul's old question suddenly sounds quite challenging again.

This chapter deals with the Cross of Christ and its implications for any Christian community that both receives candidates for initiation and tries to live what it preaches. (In chapter 5, we will develop the theology of the Cross as the major Pauline symbol for Christian initiation.) Any theology of initiation must begin with the saving action of Christ that is fleshed out in disciple groups of Christians. Several important corollaries flow from the impact of the message of the Cross on the Christian community: its shared values, its sense of the sacred, and its need to witness community. To begin this discussion, we turn to the question of what we call Jesus.

Names or Titles?

There is a difference between a name and a title. The same person may be called "Margaret Thatcher" or "Prime Minister," "George Appleton" or "Dr. Appleton," but the title is not the name. A title, unless it is purely honorific, describes the role and function of a person. One person may have several titles. In real life, however, it is important that we live up to the titles we have whether they be "father," "teacher," "mother," "son," or "daughter."

Initiation is the process of becoming part of the community of Jesus Christ. With his name comes a title, "Son of the living God" (Matt. 16:16). That title is important, not only because it describes what Jesus is and does, but also what his community should be like. In theological terms, we say christology affects our understanding of ecclesiology. In other words, the kind of Christ we have affects the kind of Church we have. There are several important titles given to Jesus in New Testament that attempt to depict the various complementary aspects of Jesus' saving work among us— prophet, Messiah, Son of Man, Lord, Son of the living God. Like a theological boomerang, however, these titles always return to the community that claims Jesus as its own. Such titles challenge the credibility and vision of that community.

Those who consider themselves Christian or are thinking of becoming Christian can learn a great deal from a scene in Matthew's gospel that deals, among other things, with titles. In chapter 16 of his gospel, Matthew selectively follows the outline of chapter 8 in Mark's gospel: a warning about the Pharisees, Peter's confession of Jesus, and a prediction of Jesus' sufferings. Because Matthew has a different theological focus than Mark, he does not, as a rule, simply repeat Mark's accounts, but reshapes or enlarges them to fit his perspective. His sixteenth chapter not only illustrates this point, but provides us with an important lesson on the titles of Christ and Peter.

In Mark's account, Peter, in response to the question "Who do you say that I am?" answers, "You are the Messiah" (Mark 8:29). In Matthew's account, however, Peter adds the title "the son of the living God" (Matt. 16:16). Unlike Mark's version, Jesus then gives a title to Peter: "I for my part declare to you, you are 'Rock,' and on this rock I will build my church" (Matt. 16:18). "Rock" or Peter (the Aramaic *kêfā* or Greek *petros*) was not a proper name in the first century A.D.[1] In effect, then, Matthew describes Jesus and Peter giving titles to one another.

But titles are never fully appreciated when taken out of context. Matthew helps us avoid that pitfall by rounding out his chapter with the prediction of Christ's sufferings in a somewhat different version than that of Mark. In the first gospel, Peter tries to dissuade Jesus from such a future; "God forbid that any such thing ever happen to you!" (Matt. 16:22). Jesus responds with a new title for Peter. The Greek text reads literally, "You are a stone of stumbling (*skandalon*) for me" (Matt. 16:23).[2] Peter now appears to have two titles, "Rock" and "stone of stumbling." Although there are many other important elements in this Matthaean scene, let us restrict our discussion to the titles of Jesus and Peter, and their meaning for the Church.[3]

In Mark's story, the title of Jesus as "Messiah" is coupled with his suffering. Peculiar to Matthew's gospel is his concern with the end-time (eschatology) and its bearing on being the Church of Christ until that time.[4] This concern influences his version of the scene that we are discussing. Just as Jesus' title "Son of the living God" is framed by his approaching suffering, so Peter's title "Rock" is more realistically understood in comparison with his other title, "stone of stumbling."

Peter, in his unique position among his fellow disciples, is a model for the church. He can acknowledge the true identity of Jesus as "Son" and yet can be "scandalized" because the title indicates what Jesus does for us—suffer and die. An earlier saying of Matthew resonates with this teaching: "No pupil outranks his teacher, no slave his master. The pupil should be glad to become like the teacher, the slave like his master" (Matt. 10:24–25). G. Bornkamm summarizes the Petrine lesson of Matthew 16 in this way: "The Church after Easter with its life and the office of the keys sanctioned by Jesus, is thus subjected to the law of the life and suffering of the earthly Jesus."[5]

As if to round out this teaching, Matthew, in recounting Jesus' walk to the Mount of Olives after the Last Supper, reverses roles. Jesus may well become the *skandalon*, the stone of stumbling, for his disciples: "Tonight you will stumble (using the verb form *skandalizein*) because of me" (Matt. 26:31). Peter, in his overconfident response, denies that he will "stumble" because of his Master (Matt. 26:33).[6] In his denial of the Master, Peter does stumble momentarily. Yet Peter still becomes "Rock" for the church and a model of the disciple who has heard Jesus' words and tried to live them: "If a man wishes to come after me, he must deny his very self, take up his cross, and begin to follow in my footsteps" (Matt. 16:24).[7]

Through the centuries, Peter has remained an appealing figure of discipleship, and therefore a model of initiation. He learns to accept Jesus as "Son of the living God" and "the one who must suffer." Jesus' strong reprimand to Peter ("Get out of my sight, you satan!" Matt. 16:23) is balanced by the disciple's postresurrection response ("You know that I love you," John 21:15) to his Master's questioning.[8] In effect, Peter learns to enlarge his definition of who Jesus, the Christ, really is and becomes a model of what the church must be and of what discipleship entails.

As in the case of Peter, the initiated and the uninitiated always have a great deal to learn about titles of Jesus and of his followers.

As in the case of Peter, we tend to be selective in titles that we apply to Christ, for if we follow a crucified Lord, can disciples be greater than the Master? Sometimes, like Peter, disciples may be tempted to evade the message of the Cross. That is why this first chapter on initiation deals with the Cross and the type of church and sacred witness it begets.

The Challenge of the Cross

At a party or a business meeting, introductions can be very important. Our first impressions of peoples' appearances and conversations are sometimes our most lasting ones. It is with some shock, then, that we see how Paul presents Jesus to his contemporaries: "As for myself . . . when I came to you I did not come proclaiming God's testimony with particular eloquence or 'wisdom.' No, I determined that while I was with you I would speak of *nothing but Jesus Christ and him crucified*" (1 Cor. 2:1–2).

To stare at a crucifix or to make the sign of the cross is not necessarily to have Paul's experience of a crucified Lord. Even twentieth-century non-Christians are accustomed to the image of a crucified Jesus from a walk through any museum filled with Medieval figures or Renaissance paintings of the crucifixion. Although the artist may have dramatically portrayed the suffering and violence of the Good Friday scene, the onlooker is still distanced from any personal involvement or commitment.

To appreciate the shock of a crucified Jesus, as did Paul's contemporaries, we must turn to an earlier age. Justin Martyr in the second century, for example, sums up the reaction of many of his pagan contemporaries to a crucified savior in one word—"insanity."[9] A hundred years earlier, Paul cites the current opinion about the Cross—"complete absurdity" (1 Cor. 1:18).

The challenge of initiation, as we have already suggested, begins with the infamy, the absurdity of the Cross. But, as we learned from Paul's opening remarks in his first letter to the Corinthians, the "word of the Cross" (1 Cor. 1:18) is to be found within a certain type of community. This community can be called "Christian" or "Church" because it has been shaped by the Cross and is indeed the "likeness to his death" (Rom. 6:5). If there are problems with the meaning and celebration of baptism and eucharist in the community, Paul has learned to look for the underlying reason—the avoidance of the Cross and its meaning.

Initiation into Christianity always takes place within a gathering of imperfect people who, sustained by the unearned strength and vision of God, learn the meaning of Christ's Cross so that they may welcome his resurrection. But even this theological description of an imperfect pastoral situation can often seem idealistic. More specifically, one might ask: Have we replaced the "word of the Cross" with crucifixes in our churches? Is the average Christian really a more active participant in the Cross of Christ than the museum visitor looking at the painting of the crucifixion by an El Greco or a Caravaggio? How much is our own Christian community learning from the Cross these days?

In a sense, such questions originate in Paul's insistent teaching that we were baptized into Christ's death (Rom. 6:3–4). Over the centuries, this Pauline teaching has sometimes been reduced to the pious practice of making the stations of the Cross or to moralizing about "death to self." But one suspects that Paul means much more than this as he keeps turning to the Cross of Christ for so much of his pastoral teaching to the Christian communities of his time.

Initiation challenges us to a very specific form of conversion that deals with the strength or weaknesses of our lived experience. But conversion is crowned by sharing in the resurrection of Christ. The foundation for any discussion of "walking" the Christian path of conversion begins with Paul's own experience of discovering the meaning of the Cross.

Paul and the Cross

Unlike Peter, John, or Mary Magdalene, Paul had not seen Christ crucified on Calvary. In fact, Paul met a risen Lord on the road to Damascus who, as a violator of the Law, had died an accursed death but now was glorified.[10] In Paul's case, the shock of conversion was connected to his love of "Jewish observance far beyond most of my contemporaries, in my excess of zeal to live out all the traditions of my ancestors" (Gal. 1:14). In persecuting the followers of the malefactor Jesus, Paul discovered he was persecuting a

risen Lord; "Who are you, sir?" he asked. The voice answered,
"I am Jesus, the one you are persecuting" (Acts 9:5). The core of
Paul's critique about false wisdom and self-justification through the
Law, as well as his emphasis on the Cross, begins with this expe-
rience. Paul's meeting with a risen Lord cast new light on the
importance of the Cross.[11]

When Paul began his Christian training, the early Christian
communities already had a number of traditional ways of expressing
the meaning of the Cross.[12] Paul repeats some of these formulas in
his own writings: "I handed on to you first of all what I myself
received, that Christ died for our sins in accordance with the
Scriptures; that he was buried and, in accordance with the Scriptures, rose on the third day" (1 Cor. 15:3–4). As Ernst Käsemann
comments, "Paul was only able to understand and preach the cross
in the light of manisfestation of the risen Lord."[13] Paul's later
pastoral experience, however, taught him that Christians sometimes
concentrated on a risen Lord to avoid the costly teaching of the
Cross. As we shall see, this temptation is always present in Christian communities.

Two words in Paul's writings capture this fear of the Cross of
Christ and its consequences—"scandal" and "foolishness." The
word "scandal" is more complex in Greek (*skandalon*) than its
English translation might suggest. The Greek word includes such
meanings as "stumbling stone" (that we saw employed so effectively in Matt. 16), "trap," "temptation," and something which
causes revulsion or arouses opposition.[14] Paul uses "scandal" and
"foolishness" (Greek: *mōria*) to sum up the attitudes of some of
his contemporaries about the Cross: "we preach Christ crucified—
a stumbling block (*skandalon*) to the Jews, and an absurdity (*mōrian*) to Gentiles" (1 Cor. 1:23).

More specifically, there is a certain group among the Corinthian
Christians whose "wisdom" blinds them to the meaning of the
Cross of Christ. More recent scholarship has concentrated on the
actual beliefs of this group.[15] For our purposes, it suffices to
describe such "wise" people as those who dismiss the Cross as
the heart of God's definition of salvation. Paul takes this challenge
of the "wise" seriously. In a carefully constructed passage,[16] Paul
contrasts God's wisdom and the "wisdom of this world" (1 Cor.

1:20): "The message of the cross is complete absurdity (*mōria*) to those who are headed for ruin, but to us who are experiencing salvation it is the power of God. Scripture says, 'I will destroy the wisdom of the wise and thwart the cleverness of the clever.' . . . Yes, Jews demand "signs' and Greeks look for 'wisdom', but we preach Christ crucified—a stumbling block (*skandalon*) to Jews, and an absurdity (*mōrian*) to Gentiles" (1 Cor. 1:18–19, 22–23).

The false wisdom that Paul attacks is an attitude, not an intellectual position.[17] Behind such an attitude are some deep assumptions about what it means to be saved and how God works. To make the point more forcefully, Paul once more plays off the word *mōria*: "For God's folly (*mōron*) is wiser than men, and his weakness more powerful than men" (1 Cor. 1:25). Confronted with the meaning of the Cross, Paul can only conclude that our faith must rest on the power of God and not on the "wisdom" of our world (1 Cor. 2:5). Since the Cross is the visible symbol of God's meaning and power, it is the ultimate criterion by which Christian faith is judged.

Like a Slave

The fact that we have not yet spoken much of the resurrection may seem somewhat surprising. The reader must keep in mind Paul's pastoral predicament. Some Christians seemed to have missed the essential sequence—death/resurrection—in the proclamation of the good news. As Peter Stuhlmacher notes, "The Risen One is preached by Paul as the crucified one."[18] After all, our natural inclination is toward security and glory, and not toward suffering and death.

Notice, then, how Paul speaks to a typical Christian community that he had founded. He attempts to encourage and strengthen them as a community: "Conduct yourselves, then, in a way worthy of the gospel of Christ. . . . Make my joy complete by your unanimity, possessing the one love, united in spirit and ideals . . . each of you looking to others' interests rather than his own" (Phil. 1:27; 2:2, 4). Paul than fleshes out the attitude that will realize these ideals by recalling a familiar Christian hymn.[19]

This hymn describes how Christ humbled himself and how God

glorified him as if echoing the similar Lucan text: "For everyone who exalts himself shall be humbled while he who humbles himself shall be exalted" (Luke 18:14). The hymn illustrates this humility: "He was known to be of human estate, and it was thus that he humbled himself, obediently accepting even death" (Phil. 2:7c–8). Paul then inserts his own emphasis, "death on a cross."[20] But it is the insertion of the Pauline "death on a cross" that transforms a redemption story, familiar to any pagan, into a unique account of Jesus' self-gift.[21]

Jesus' death in the letter to the Philippians is described as an "obedience" that is freely given. To appreciate this insight, recall the Passion accounts. In them Jesus submits himself freely to those forces of evil that people have no control over. Like the too familiar, contemporary accounts of the tortured and persecuted of some countries, Jesus is vulnerable to injustice and its final weapon, death.

This same theme of the Cross understood as a freely given obedience appears in the letter to the Hebrews: "Since therefore the children share in blood and flesh, *he himself participated in them*, in order that through death he might abrogate him who has the power of death, that is, the devil, *and deliver those who, in fear of death, were all of their lives bound in slavery*" (Heb. 2:14–15). In other words, Jesus suffered the same inhuman degradation that continues to rob so many of their human dignity and destiny. Jesus' "participation" in our common situation changes everything.[22] This is, in fact, the Jesus of the letter to the Hebrews: "tempted in every way that we are, yet never sinned" (Heb. 4:15).

The importance of describing Jesus as an "obedient, crucified one" is only appreciated if sin is understood as radical disobedience. Paul returns to this idea more than once. Just as an original disobedience wrought havoc on the course of human history, so Jesus' unique obedience made possible a radically new relation with God (Rom. 5:18–19). The Cross as the symbol of free, loving obedience is, in fact, God's announcement of his new creation.[23]

Neither Jew nor Gentile expected the solution of the Cross: a free and radical "yes" given by Jesus. For some people the Cross would always be associated with shame, crime, and loss of human dignity. No wonder that the "wise" called the solution of the Cross "foolish.'' But there are more subtle ways for Christians to react in precisely the same manner, as the Corinthian situation shows. Under a veneer of Christianity, there have always been some ''wise'' people who know that the Cross was an unnecessary detour to resurrection.

Saved from What?

The attitude of ''law and order'' carried to an extreme can turn a law-abiding person into a violator of the law. Such a person has usually forgotten the purpose of the law. Victor Hugo, in his famous nineteenth-century novel *Les Misérables*, employs this psychological insight with great skill. The police commissioner relentlessly pursues a former thief, Jean Valjean, because the latter has not sufficiently expiated his petty crime. In doing so, the police commissioner becomes a greater criminal, eventually destroyed by his conviction that goodness is the perfect observance of the law.

The first surprising result of the Cross for Paul is freedom from the law. Paul uses the term ''law,'' of course, in a very precise way. Historically, the human story, in fact, has been one of disobedience. Actually, the law only seems to have reinforced our persistent tendency to rebel. Paul's assessment of this age-old story is that ''by works of the law no one will be justified'' (Gal. 2:16).

But the Cross radically changed all this by becoming the dividing point between this utterly hopeless human situation of disobedience (which Paul evocatively calls ''death'') and the newly won possibility of being children of God. The Cross is the symbol of Jesus' obedience, an obedience never achieved by the law. Through his obedience, we are now enabled, in turn, to be obedient. This new possibility is the sheer gift of God. But Paul has learned from difficult pastoral experience that Christians could refuse this gift and try once again to ''earn'' salvation by observance of the law.

The Galatian Christians are a good example of the problem. They seem tempted to forget that God's salvation is not achieved by ''doing'' certain things (in this case, getting circumcised). Paul knows that this situation could only arise because the message of the Cross has not yet been fully learned: ''You senseless Galatians! Who has cast a spell over you—you before whose eyes Jesus Christ was displayed to view upon his cross?'' (Gal. 3:1).[24] Good teacher that Paul is, he cites the book of Deuteronomy (21.23) in an unexpected way to reteach the lesson of the Cross: ''Christ has delivered us from the power of the law's curse by himself becoming a curse for us, as it is written: 'Accursed is anyone who is hanged on a tree' '' (Gal. 3:13).[25] This is the paradox of the Cross: the accursed one is the liberator of his brothers and sisters.

The Cross in Paul's own experience is the only means to escape from the situation that ''law'' (that is, the good conduct that we mistakenly think earns us the ''right'' to God's love) creates. Paul's conversion had taught him this basic truth. Recalling his earlier days, Paul admits ''in legal observance I was a Pharisee, and so zealous that I persecuted the church. I was above reproach when it came to justice based on the law'' (Phil. 3:5–6). The law, on the other hand, increases our offense because we always fail to perform perfectly (Rom. 5:20). The beginning of salvation is learning to accept the gift we did not and cannot earn—the self-gift of Christ on the Cross: ''You died to the law through the body of Christ, that you might belong to that Other who was raised from the dead, so that we might bear fruit for God'' (Rom. 7:4).[26]

None of these discussions about the Cross and the law was academic as far as Paul was concerned. On the contrary, these Pauline teachings originated in the pastoral problems of his ministry. The continuing obstacle to welcoming the message of the Cross among the candidates and the baptized of a twentieth century Christian community remains the same as that of Paul's time: the unwillingness to believe that salvation cannot be earned and that Christ's self-gift is the only model by which we can learn to be obedient to the law of love.

Paul is leading up to the meaning of faith, a relationship in which we become sons and daughters of God in Christ (Gal. 3:26). This ability to believe is grounded in God's unearned love that touches our own experience from the beginning. Paul, the former Pharisee, describes the difference that justification and faith have made in his life: ''I have been crucified with Christ, and the life I live now is not my own; Christ is living in me. I still live my human life, but it is a life of faith in the Son of God, who loved me and gave himself for me. . . . *If justice is available through the law, then*

Christ died to no purpose!'' (Gal. 2:19–21). This last line remains one of the strongest challenges of the gospel proclamation. In a society such as ours, which sometimes teaches its children to be excessively competitive and overachieving, the startling nature of salvation as unearned gift is not an easy lesson to learn.

I have described justification elsewhere as God going before us in our experience.[27] God's loving initiative of rescuing us, as symbolized in the Cross of Christ, is not a theoretical statement but rather an experience which each person, like Paul, discovers and welcomes time and again. The Galatians had once believed this, but now, as Paul's letter to them attests, they are forgetting the gratuitous ways in which God strengthened them. The Cross has once again become a "stumbling block" (Gal. 5:11).

How does the Cross become a stumbling stone even in the lives of those who seemed quite committed to the Christian way of life? We cannot answer the question without reviewing the Pauline connections already presented. The Cross is the symbol of Jesus' redemptive attitude—obedience. In contrast, sin with the help of the law is radical disobedience to God's vision and meaning of creation and of our place in it. The Cross is the door to faith because it sums up God's meaning, Christ's obedience, and our participation in the new creation. As in Paul's case, however, the meaning of the Cross is worked out against the landscape of our lives, in the banal and dramatic events that always bring troubling questions about what we think is really going on.

Because we do not always make the same practical connections Paul makes, the Cross can become a stumbling stone without our realizing it. Much of our American cultural identity, for example, has been shaped by the ideal of "earning our own way." In our personal lives, self-achievement and independence usually form part of our personality profile. When the feelings, the events, or the unexpected crises of our lives threaten our self-made worlds, we may still "say our prayers" and receive eucharist without ever seeing the connection between the Cross and the current chapter of our lives. To accept God's unearned strength and a new lesson on the purpose of our lives is the practical test of whether the Cross is the door to faith at this particular stage of our lives. On a communal level, a local parish may distribute sacraments, consolation, and material help to its members without ever being challenged by the theology of the Cross about its current priorities or praxis.

This is why Paul's challenge to the Galatians is so astounding even nineteen hundred years later. As F. F. Bruce notes, citing Cicero, the word Cross was "unmentionable in polite Roman society."[28] Yet Paul prays, "May I never boast of anything but the Cross of our Lord Jesus Christ! Through it, the world has been crucified to me and I to the world. It means nothing whether one is circumcised or not. All that matters is that one is created anew" (Gal. 6:14–15). Translated into contemporary language, the Cross gives a unique sense of direction and purpose in life that results in a new world here and hereafter.

Whose Sufferings?

Most Christians' natural inclination would be to stare at the events of Jesus' suffering and death in much the same way that a tourist views Michelangelo's *Pièta*. The viewer sees a depiction of the sorrowing Mary holding the crucified corpse of Jesus in her lap. The tourist's reactions may range from an appreciation of Michelangelo's art to some religious emotion. Such reactions, however, are not what Paul had in mind when he speaks about *participation* in the sufferings of Christ.

In a typical passage Paul explains how the death of Jesus is now his death: "Continually we carry about in our bodies the dying of Jesus, so that in our bodies the life of Jesus may be revealed" (2 Cor. 4:10). Ever since Paul's world was turned upside down by his conversion experience on the road to Damascus, his story has been one of committed struggle and patient suffering for the sake of the Gospel. If Paul had remained a Pharisee, he would not have had to endure a hard life nor a violent death.

The "dying of Jesus" is not a striking metaphor for Paul but a process that entails practical consequences in his daily living. The connection between Jesus' death and his own life-struggle is so strong that Paul uses the same Greek verb to describe his experience as is used of Jesus' passion: "While we live we are constantly *being delivered to death* for Jesus' sake" (2 Cor. 4:11).[29]

Paul is not content to leave the matter there. Participation in the sufferings and death of Jesus is characteristic, in Paul's mind, of the Christian disciple.[30] *The first practical corollary of this theology of the Cross is a life spent for the sake of others*: "He died for all so that those who live might live no longer for themselves" (2 Cor. 5:15). The new Christian vision about the meaning of life also requires a reevaluation of how we intend to use the remaining time and resources of this life. For Paul, the Cross provides a radically new focus on living and dying that he is ready to illustrate from his own experience and priorities.

The second corollary derived from Paul's teaching on participation in the death of Jesus is based on this new orientation: *personal and communal values and priorities must be constantly reassessed*. What had been important in Paul's life up to the moment of his conversion had changed significantly. Paul now measures everything by Christ. In summing up what he has altered in his life, the apostle uses the financial language of his day in picturing a balance sheet of assets and liabilities, of gain and loss.[31] "But those things I used to consider gain I have now reappraised as loss in the light of Christ. . . . For his sake I have forfeited everything; I have accounted all else rubbish so that Christ may be my wealth" (Phil. 3:7-8).

From the edited outlines of Paul's life in Acts or from his own autobiographical remarks, for example, in 2 Corinthians, it is easy to verify the apostle's claim that he had "shared much in the suffering of Christ" (2 Cor. 1:5). Paul's apostolic life could be superficially analyzed as that of a driven man. But motivation is a key factor in interpreting a person's experience. The source of Paul's strength is the meaning of the Cross and the overriding desire to share in the self-gift of Jesus. This is the only way to share also in the resurrection (Phil. 3:10-11). But Paul's heroic generosity and commitment to the Gospel may appear so intimidating that it does not seem applicable to ordinary lives.

The Strength of the Weak

In response to this fear we can add a third practical corollary, based on Paul's theology of the Cross: *the weak are made strong through the Cross*. Once again, Paul begins with the lesson of the

Cross: "He was crucified out of weakness, but he lives by the power of God" (2 Cor. 13:4). As Georg Eichholz has suggested, our assumptions about God are corrected by the Cross on which the weakness of God shines forth as a new definition of power.[32] In fact, this is a variation on the Pauline theme, discussed earlier, of God's "foolishness" (1 Cor. 1:25). In Paul's own conversion experience, to look on a crucified Lord is to see God in a startling new way.

"Weakness," then, is not a pejorative term for Paul. The Cross has taught him to deal with weakness in his own life, as a careful reading of 2 Corinthinians proves. Paul found himself in a difficult pastoral situation in which his own apostleship was seriously questioned by some "pseudoapostles" (2 Cor. 11:13) at Corinth.[33]

In chapter 11 of this second letter to the Corinthians, Paul recounts some of the suffering his apostolic witness has caused him (2 Cor. 11:23–28). This is followed by an autobiographical reference to an ecstatic experience fourteen years earlier and to "a thorn in the flesh, a Satan to beat me" (2 Cor. 12:7). For the purposes of our present discussion, Paul's summary of what he learned from trying to deal with this vaguely described problem in his life is important. After praying to be relieved of this problem, God's answer to Paul turns on the words "weak" and "power": "My grace is enough for you, for in weakness power reaches perfection" (2 Cor. 12:9).

The lesson of the Cross taught Paul how the weakness of Christ is the source of strength for the Christian. As C. K. Barrett correctly notes, the "weakness" of Christ is seen in Jesus' identification with the marginal and outcast people of his society (tax collectors, prostitutes, and so forth) long before the event of the Cross.[34] This vulnerability and poorness of Jesus is, in Paul's teaching, both a source of encouragement and a model: "for your sake he (Christ) made himself poor though he was rich, so that you might become rich by his poverty" (2 Cor. 8:9).

The Church of the Weak

A fourth corollary to Paul's teaching on the Cross is the logical conclusion to his discussion on participation in the sufferings of

Christ: *the Christian community, the Church, is characterized by its sharing in the sufferings of the Lord Jesus.* When Paul hears of the sufferings of the Thessalonian Christians, for example, he reminds them how these sufferings identity them with their fellow Christians in Palestine who, like Jesus, endure much (1 Thess. 2:14–15). But there are more profound reasons than common sufferings that prompt Paul to call Jesus "the first-born of many brothers and sisters" (Rom. 8:29). Although we will discuss the connection between baptism into the death of Jesus (Rom. 6:4) and the community as the body of Christ in chapter 5, it is important that we begin to see how Christ's self-gift results in a community marked by the Cross. Such a connection is of more than academic interest for contemporary Christian communities since they are still measured by the way the Cross changes the ways they should live, worship, and work together.

There is one kind of world that no Christian community could survive in—a world in which everyone is a slave to sin, a world in which, as we saw above, the law tripped us up rather than helped us. Paul sets up a comparison between the kind of world that existed before and after the Cross. In effect, the Cross is the boundary line between two dominions or reigns. Like refugees from a devastated and tyrannized land who cross the borders into a promising and free country, so Christians pass from death to life, from law to freedom, from offense to justice: "To sum up, then: just as a single offense brought condemnation to all men, a single righteous act brought all men acquittal and life" (Rom. 5:18).[35] This single righteous act is, of course, Jesus' death.

The "reign of death" was a losing situation that only aggravated the problem of human responsibility. People contributed to this flawed context by their own selfishness, wilfullness, and destructiveness. Paul makes the connection between one person's ("Adam") sin and "death thus *coming to all men inasmuch as all sinned*" (Rom. 5:12).[36] The practical corollary of this hopeless scene is that one person's sin effectively keeps that person isolated from others. It is as if Paul were describing a world in which everyone was quarantined. In such a world, community would be impossible. But with the Cross this cosmic hopelessness has been changed.

Any twentieth-century person surveying his or her world might think that Paul is cruelly mistaken. In a world of international distrust, widespread famine and poverty, and systematic torture and injustice, we might wonder if Paul's conviction is warranted. In other words, has anything radically changed since the first person's sin? Paul's answer, a resounding "yes," is summed up in a phrase—"us along with you in Christ" (2 Cor. 1:21). With freedom as the gift of the Cross comes the community of the free, the Church.

The New Community

Paul was accustomed to dealing with imperfect Christian communities, as we have noted. In fact, their misunderstanding of or conflict with his teaching on participation in the sufferings of Christ seem to have occasioned a development of Paul's own thinking on the subject. People prefer, after all, to deal with a glorified Christ who is less challenging and more comforting as a model than with a crucified Lord.[37]

For Paul, one visible proof of the new world Christ had ushered in was the Christian community, the "body of Christ." Although Christians in such a community were by no means sinless, they had begun to come together in new ways in Christ. Paul's world was still haunted by social, economic, and personal oppression, but he remained convinced that the Church as a community "in Christ" made a crucial difference in human history.

Paul depicts Christ and the Christian community in surprising ways: "Do you not see that your bodies are members of Christ?" (1 Cor. 6:15). As J. Murphy-O'Connor points out, Paul speaks of the community as Christ, presuming the identification familiar to his readers.[38] Later, in the same letter to the Corinthians, he sums up the analogy of the Church as one body and many members in the same way: "so it is with Christ" (1 Cor. 12:12).[39] In other words, Christ and the community form one reality. (In chapter 5, we will discuss a related idea of the Christian "in Christ.") In this identification of Christ and Christians, Paul is not describing the baptized as sinless or saviors like Christ. Rather, he is pinpointing the radically new possibility of those who die with Christ: they will bear a family resemblance to the one they follow.

We find the implications of those connections brought out again in two letters which, if not of Pauline authorship, are certainly familiar with this theology. The writer of the letter to the Ephesians reminds his readers of what Christ's self-gift has changed in their lives: "You who once were far off have been brought near through the blood of Christ. It is he who is our peace, and who made the two of us one by *breaking down the barrier of hostility that kept us apart*" (Eph. 2:13–14). This is the practical result of reconciliation through the Cross: we are no longer aliens but "fellow citizens of the saints and members of the household of God" (Eph. 2:19).

The Cross does not bring us into an elitist club of the saved, but rather into the company of participants in Christ's work. After speaking of reconciliation through the Cross,[40] the writer to the Colossians startles us with this challenge: "Even now I find my joy in the suffering I endure for you. In my own flesh I fill up what is lacking in the sufferings of Christ for the sake of his body, the church" (Col. 1:24). This sentence could be easily misinterpreted to mean that Christ's self-gift on the Cross was imperfect. In the context, however, the message of Colossians is clear: we must do our part in living and proclaiming this unearned gift of Christ.[41] Christians are those who have moved from a passive helplessness before the evil still rampant in this world to an active imitation of Christ: "For this I work and struggle, impelled by that energy of his which is so powerful a force within me" (Col. 1:29). The theory behind such participation is inviting, but what is the dynamic behind such unified witness?

Like-Minded Communities

Paul entertains high hopes for the imperfect Christian communities of his time. These hopes are captured in one Greek verb that he uses fairly often—*phronein*. The word can be translated in several ways, but a general Pauline meaning for *phronein* is "to set one's mind on" or "to be of one mind/heart." When Paul uses this verb, he means not only thinking alike, but also feeling united by common purposes and shared goals.[42] In Paul's pastoral experience, the key to becoming authentic Christian communities is contained in the effort to share a common vision, shaped by the gospel proclamation.

To understand this, we turn to the letter to the Philippians where Paul employs *phronein* most often. Here is a typical passage: "make my joy complete by your unanimity (*tò autò phronēte*), possessing the one love, united in spirit (*phronountes*), and ideals. . . . Your attitude must be that of Christ (*phroneite*)" (Phil. 2:1–2, 5).[43] A reader unfamiliar with Greek can still perceive the difficult task of the translator in trying to render into English the many nuances of *phronein* as used three times in these lines.

The Greek-speaking world of Paul's time was familiar with different types of religious communities. The community of the "mystery" religions, for example, was outwardly quite similar to the Christian community in some respects. Its candidates were initiated into cultic practices. Unlike the Christian communities, however, these pagan communities did not share a way of life and a future vision, but only rituals of worship.[44] In Philippians 2, Paul is describing a like-minded group of people, though drawn from all strata of society, and possessing widely varying social and educational backgrounds.[45] A Christian community in Paul's view must be characterized by an inner transforming purpose that sets it apart from other models of community.[46] J. P. Sampley sums up this Pauline teaching in this way: "Christians come together not because of some social club mentality. Rather Christians share this: God's love was shown to them while they were all sinners, helpless."[47]

Paul gives a practical example of *phronein* later in the same letter to the Philippians: "I plead with Evodia just as I do with Syntyche: come to some mutual understanding (*autò phronein*) in the Lord" (Phil. 4:2). Whatever the point of tension between these Christians was, Paul reminds them of a common foundation—Jesus Christ. They have shared in the labors of the Gospel with Paul. Now they are called upon to share in deeper ways. Paul urges Christians to this same effort elsewhere—"to live in perfect harmony with one another (*tò autò phronein*) according to the spirit of Jesus Christ" (Rom. 15:5).[48]

Paul had found that the myopic self-concern of some Christians made community difficult: "Everyone is busy seeking his own interests rather than those of Christ Jesus" (Phil. 2:21). Participation in the cultic practices of the mystery religion communities required no deeper commitments to fellow worshippers. Each one was, in fact, free to pursue his or her own interests. Paul, however, insisted on spelling out the consequences of the Cross for living together as Christians.

Community, as Bernard Lonergan reminds us, is built on common meanings that are achieved through decisions and choices.[49] The meaning of the Cross in Paul's theology profoundingly questions why we do what we do. In other words, the best contemporary synonym for Paul's *phronein* or like-mindedness is intentionality, a topic we will discuss more fully in chapter 3. Intentionality includes the focus we give our lives, the meanings we cling to, and the decisions we make. For the moment it will suffice to make certain connections between the Cross and intentionality.

Good intentions in Christian living are those that have been shaped by and measured against Christ's self-gift on the Cross. When people begin to allow the meaning of the Cross to challenge their cherished options and life-decisions, then a sharing of meaning and the renewal of authentic community occurs. For our intentions always affect the way we live and walk with others. Just as Paul can describe some Christians as enemies of the Cross because of their values and intentions (Phil. 3:18–19), so another Pauline writer can urge honest Christians: "Be intent on (*phroneite*) things above rather than on things of earth" (Col. 3:2). There is no better way to illustrate how the intentions of Christians can unify or destroy community than to examine how God's Word challenged seven church communities in the book of Revelation.

"A Word to the Churches"

To be Christian together has never been easy. We sometimes forget this because we confuse our cultural and familiar background as Christians with the New Testament descriptions of Christian community. It is still not uncommon, for example, for Catholics growing up in Brooklyn or Philadelphia to identify their neighborhood by their parish: "I'm from Holy Name!" For some people, Christian identity within a parish is limited to growing up with certain friends who are Catholics, or to a set of buildings we call "our parish," or to being a graduate of a parochial school. In other words, in the experience of many Christians, "church" means a building, or an international organization that they belong to, or a set of autobiographical stories that form part of their cultural, ethnical, or familiar background as an Irish Catholic from Brooklyn, a Polish or Italian Catholic from Chicago or Buffalo.

If readers need a reminder of the difficulty of being an authentic Christian community, they might review the opening chapters of the last book of the New Testament, the book of Revelation. In a highly stylized but provocative manner, the writer confronts seven communities that lay along the same Roman road in Asia Minor.[50] Against two churches the writer had no complaint—"I know of your tribulation and your poverty, even though you are rich" (Rev. 2:9). But there is a mixture of praise and blame for the other Christian communities. The church at Ephesus is told: "I know your deeds, your labors, and your patient endurance. . . . I hold this against you, though: you have turned aside from your early love" (Rev. 2:2,4). The church at Sardis hears equally pointed words: "I know the reputation you have of being alive when in fact you are dead! Wake up, and strengthen what remains before it dies" (Rev. 3:1–2). But the words addressed to the church at Laodicea are the most unforgettable: "I know your deeds; I know you are neither hot nor cold. . . . But because you are lukewarm, neither hot nor cold, I will spew you out of my mouth" (Rev. 3:15–16).

Certainly, the church communities in Asia Minor were plagued with a variety of problems: difficulties of being Christian in their public lives, sporadic persecution from the Jewish communities, and internal heresy and dissent.[51] But like an ostinato theme, reiterated incessantly, each vision-prophecy to a community ends with the words: "Let him who has ears heed the Spirit's word to the churches!" (for example, Rev. 2:7). In brief, prophetic warnings and teachings are once more needed to transform groups of people into communities of Christians.[52]

Theologies of Church do not create such communities. Long before Vatican II, the pioneering theological work of H. DeLubac, Y. Congar, K. Rahner, and many others prepared the way for that council's stirring statements on the Church. In sharp contrast to previous manual theology, Vatican II retrieved the biblical notions of Church as community, and of Christians as "the holy people of God": "in this way the Church simultaneously prays and labors in order that the entire world may become the People of God, the

Body of the Lord, and the Temple of the Holy Spirit, and that in Christ, the Head of all, there may be rendered to the Creator and the Father of the Universe all honor and glory."[53]

As in the case of the seven churchs of Asia Minor, there are a number of internal and external reasons why today's Christian communities, if they listen attentively, will still hear the familiar prophetic warning: "let him who has ears heed the Spirit's word to the churches!" In addition to the obvious sociological question about whether the typical parish structure represents an outmoded and unrealistic way of gathering and caring for large groups of people in our posturban American society, there are the more practical aspects of the prophetic warning to contend with: the function of the inner-city parish in a largely "nonpracticing" neighborhood, the relation of parochical schools to the mission of their parishes, decreasing financial resources and ministerial personnel, the conscious and unconscious preservation of middle-class social attitudes by some parishes, and ultimately, the fear of the gospel challenge to underlying social and personal assumptions and values.

Two decades after Vatican II, there are also deeper theological questions about the actual praxis in local communities of Christians that we call our "diocese" or "parish." The term "praxis," of course, refers to the specific situation and activities of a particular group of Christians, in contrast to their theories about "church." P. Murnion, has pinpointed five troubled areas of parish praxis that have important theological ramifications: (1) expressing the mysteries of faith; (2) the nature of the Church community; (3) person and role in the Church; (4) shared responsibility; and (5) the relationship between Church and society.[54]

The pastoral dimension of these areas is reflected in specific questions such as "Does the sacramental experience of this parish give it a sense of mission to anyone?" and "Do we have to follow the moral leadership of the bishops on questions of abortion but not on nuclear disarmament?" If the author of the book of Revelations were addressing, for example, the church at San Francisco, New Orleans, or New York, it would again be on the basis of a troubled praxis that did not correspond with the gospel teaching about what an ecclesial community, called a "diocese" or "parish," should be.

The Cross and the Initiating Community

One of the earliest scenes in the book of Revelation after the warnings to the seven churches is that of a heavenly liturgy in which a central figure is the "Lamb that was slain" (Rev. 5:12). The new hymn sung to the Lamb tells how he purchased with his blood people of every race and "made of them a kingdom, and priests to serve our God" (Rev. 5:9–10).[55] In this magnificent image, the writer sums up much of our earlier discussion: the Cross begets a special type of community, united by its service of God and, therefore, honest in its worship. Although the language of this scene is liturgical, the service demanded had been previously spelled out in the practical warnings to the seven churches. This image of the Cross and its practical consequence can serve as a model for our discussion.

Of what use is it to repeat Paul's description of initiation as being baptized into the death of Christ, if there is no credible community marked by the Cross to proclaim that truth? Proclamation of the Cross and its message, after all, is not repetition of the Passion narratives, but testifying to the power of Christ's self-gift in our shared lives. We have argued that the challenge of initiation begins with the message of the Cross: *Christ's self-gift radically frees us, not to be saved privately, but to be Christ-like in this world*. Although we need the insights of the human sciences to assist us in building and analyzing the nature of a contemporary community, the starting point is the Cross. Otherwise, Christian communities can quickly degenerate into pious associations whose purpose and mission have become more socially oriented than Kingdom-bound.

No church community can escape from the social and political world it inhabits. On the other hand, every Christian community is shaped, to some extent, by the peculiar christology it lives by in praxis. R. Brown has shown, for example, the surprising diversity among New Testament house-churches and communities, both in terms of their ethnic make-up and its consequences, and in the ways they proclaimed Jesus.[56] In a similar way today, the widely different cultural contexts and operational theologies of a "basic Christian community'' in Peru, a suburban parish in Westchester, New York, and a student parish in Berkeley, California, sometimes produce widely divergent communities in terms of christology and ecclesiology. We are not speaking here of the orthodoxy (correct doctrine) of these communities, but of their orthopraxis (authentic gospel living). Yet, in two thousand years of honest effort to be the church of Christ, the constant measure of success has remained the Cross and how this norm changed the lives and mission of a particular group of people.

Until people are convinced that the message of the Cross is not, first of all, a doctrine, but a shared way of life, we will continue to have Christians who let the ''professionals,'' that is, clergy, religious education personnel, and others, worry about the life and mission of the community while the other Christians join only the Sunday worship of the community. According to Paul, this type of ecclesiology does not work in praxis. In effect, Paul teaches that such attitudes short-circuit the meaning of Jesus as savior and misinterpret the radical sin from which he rescues us. Therefore, Paul's own refusal to ''treat God's gracious gift as pointless'' (Gal. 2:21) is also a warning to Christians of each age. We did not need a crucified Lord to have rituals, meeting places, and social and cultural reenforcement. Without a crucified Lord, however, we will learn not how to be ''Rock,'' like Peter, but rather become a ''stone of stumbling'' in our own time.

The Cross and the Community's Values

Bernard Lonergan employs the phrase ''originating value'' to describe our communal and individual choices, based on what we prize. Such values color and modify our orientation to the world we live in and the contributions we make to its progress or decline.[57] I have been arguing that a theology of initiation must begin with the normative way in which Christ's death challenges and convokes the initiating community. Only in this way does the complementary teaching on the resurrection retain its full impact (a point we shall return to in later chapters). When our Christian community, on the other hand, has trouble expressing the mysteries of faith, the nature of the Church community, the individual's role in the mission of the

Church, shared responsibility and relationships between the Church and society, it would be naive to limit ourselves to sociological analyses and solutions, helpful as these may be. Rather, like the writer of the book of Revelation, we must first ask if the Cross in the actual praxis of our community is still the originating value.

One example of the Cross as an originating value in the Christian community is the morality which it evokes from its members and by which it challenges the socially structured sin of its day. This Cross-centered morality is in strong contrast to the self-serving moralities of certain Christian communities, past or present, that deal with specific personal actions but will not confront the structural evil of economic and social injustice within its own society. Paul is familiar with this problem.

In Chapter 6 of 1 Corinthians, Paul addresses some moral solutions that the Corinthians have adopted in practical matters, such as lawsuits and their sexual lives. Chapter 7 of the same letter deals with marriage, virginity, and widows. The following chapter discusses the question of meat offered to idols. Paul, in effect, reminds the community of its originating value: "When you sin thus against your brothers and wound their weak consciences, *you are sinning against Christ*" (1 Cor. 8:12). In the previous sentence, Paul had described the brother or sister as one "for whom Christ died." In chapter 6, the same value had been stated in another way; "Do you not see that your bodies are *members of Christ?*" (1 Cor. 6:15). In other words, the originating value is the Christ who gave himself for us.

From the vantage point of this value, Paul is then able to draw out its communal and personal implications in a consistent way, as well as correct the self-serving aberrations of the Corinthians. This overarching value of the Cross is, therefore, quite different from a "band-aid" morality that is incapable of reforming the deeper attitudes of the community and its awareness of its prophetic tasks in the world. Put another way, the like-mindedness (*phronein*) of Christ and Christians that the letter to the Philippians insists upon is the result of this transforming value. Our world and its problems are seen in a different light. Our particular Christian community can reexamine its mission because this value and its implications extend much further than maxims like "Be just," "Be pure," and so on, that a Stoic philosophy could have and often did suggest even before the time of Christ. The Cross gives a specificity to the moral life of the Christian community and its members.

The Cross and a Sense of the Sacred

A contemporary example of two Christian communities may help introduce us to the question of the Christian sense of the sacred. Imagine a parish in a large South American city whose members are, for the most part, from the more affluent and educated class. Some of these parishioners are military or government officials in a region notorious for violations of human rights and oppression of certain groups. The people consider themselves good Christians. They contribute to charitable causes of the diocese and follow the commandments according to their lights. These people perform sacramental rituals with respect and participate regularly in liturgical celebrations.

The second parish in the same city is in a barrio where extreme poverty, widespread illiteracy, and appalling health conditions are prevalent. Some of these people regard the Church as part of the establishment. Others who do come to the parish seem more in need of assistance than of liturgy. What religion there is among these people seems to be a mixture of superstition and resignation. The examples may seem overdrawn to some readers, but, unfortunately, missionaries usually can give specific details for both situations. But these two pastoral situations provoke a disturbing question: What is the link between the Cross as an originating value and the Christian sense of the sacred?

Both communities are characterized, for better or worse, by their sense of the sacred that animates their worship and their lives. For a group united by the meaning of the Cross, the sacred should mean much more than the ''numinous'' or a sense of awe and otherness. Such definitions and attitudes about the sacred demand only spectators. In brief, God seen as the Holy of Holies or as the Father of the crucified Jesus invites radically different views of the sacred.

The Cross introduces a profoundly new sense of the sacred into the life of a Christian community. The sacred is no longer reduced to rituals of time and space, to expiation or intercession, or to the private purposes of the community that may substitute for exigent covenantal relationships. The writer of the letter to the Hebrews teaches this new sense of the sacred in the telling metaphor of Jesus as High Priest. In several chapters, the writer systematically expands this image until he finally arrives at the heart of the matter— Jesus enters into the ritual space of the sanctuary "not with the blood of goats and calves, but with his own blood" (Heb. 9:12). The temple sanctuary is, of course, a major image for the presence of God. The sacrifice of the Cross is presented here by means of sacrificial language of the temple worship. While other sacrifices must be repeated, Jesus' self-gift is so definitive that it can "cleanse our consciences from the dead works *to worship the living God*" (Heb. 9:14).

At the center of Jesus' sacrifice is his willingness to do God's will (Heb. 10:8–10). This is why his offering in Hebrews is considered so perfect. Fulfilling the prophets' pleas for honest worship, Jesus offers a sacrifice rooted in his inmost attitudes and values. The direct result of this sacrifice is that Christians may imitate Jesus' attitude, and follow him in this same path to the sacred (Heb. 10:19). The "utter sincerity and absolute confidence" (Heb. 10:22) proposed to Christians as the doorway to the sacred is modeled on the attitudes of Jesus.

What emerges from this brief discussion is the vital connection between the Cross both as an originating value and as the origin of the Christian sense of the sacred. Although it is normal for most religions to link "worthiness" (moral or ritual) with the sacred, Christ's self-giving attitude and actions redefine the shape and purpose of our values and actions, and enlarge the sense of the sacred to include God's wider vision.

A revealing image that captures the early Christian sense of the sacred is the "orantes" figure seen on catacomb walls. The figure stands with hands uplifted. We do not need to hear the words of the figure's prayer because the cruciform posture of the praying Christian eloquently embodies the attitudes we have been discussing.[58] If one were asked how this anonymous Christian learned this sense of the sacred, one possible answer might be some form of catechumenal process in which the Cross and its corollaries were gradually unfolded. Long before political toleration allowed Christians to have churches, that is, sacred spaces, they learned a shared sense of the sacred by the ways in which they appropriate the attitude of Christ who "learned obedience from what he suffered" (Heb. 5:8).

In one way or another, then, all initiation is linked to a sense of the sacred. Both Christian worship and life must be permeated with that awareness. Unlike the anthropologist who might generally describe the sacred as "abnormal, timeless, ambiguous, at the edge,"[59] the Christian sense of the sacred is grounded in the presence of God, perceived and responded to through the power of the Cross that the Spirit mediates. Since it is the crucified Lord who bridges the gap between us and his Father, we are presented with a new view of the sacred, framed by the self-gift of Jesus. Interestingly, Paul, in arguing against "lewd conduct," brings forward the sacred image of the Christian body as the temple of the Holy Spirit (1 Cor. 6:19). In a penetrating way, he then offers what is an excellent definition of the sacred in the sense we have been describing: "You are not your own. *You have been purchased and at a price. So glorify God in your body*" (1 Cor. 6:19–20).[60] Once more, the Cross and worship are connected.

To return to our initial examples, how would the writer of the book of Revelation prophetically address the affluent and the poor of Christian communities that are apparently so different from one another? Although the warnings would be custom-tailored, no doubt, to each community, I suspect that any comment on the response of these Christians to God's presence within and outside the liturgy would again be formed by the image of the "Lamb who was slain." I am persuaded that the affluent church would be questioned about whether the neglect of the demands of the Cross had narrowed their sense of what "sacred" really means. The poorer church might be asked to reassess how the power of the Cross is the only solution God seems to have given to human-made misery. In either case, the book of Revelation's warnings about how Christian communities can delude themselves would be no less pointed today than in the first century A.D.

The Christian Community as Martyr

It is not surprising that early Christian communities, shaped by the Cross of Christ, had many martyrs. The word "martyr" means "witness." The Church has the privileged task to witness to what God is doing among us. The Cross is the highly coded symbol of God's saving action, but a shared witness must be given in each historical era to that action and its implications for a specific culture and time. The Christian community's success in preparing candidates for initiation into the death and resurrection of Christ is measured, in good part, by its ability to call out a shared witness to the message of the Cross. This is the ordinary martyrdom that any Christian community must be willing to undergo regularly.

If the Cross implies, as we have argued, a specific commitment to Christ's values and to a unique sense of the sacred, then the Christian community will have to take a close look at the culture in which this theology must be lived out. This task is more complicated than might first appear. Clifford Geertz's much cited definition of culture illustrates the point: "A historically transmitted pattern of meanings embodied in symbols . . . by means of which (persons) communicate, perpetuate, and develop their knowledge and attitudes toward life."[61] In brief, culture interprets the meanings and purposes that are vital to a group's living in a specific time and place. But if the cultural community is to be successful in handing on its heritage, it must know how to present that message in relevant ways.[62]

The Christian community's task, then, is doubly difficult. First, the values and vision of any culture will inevitably clash with the message of the Cross. This message, after all, reviews our past and present in the light of God's future. This eschatological view can give some radically different interpretations to our cultural situation than our American society, for example, does. Whenever the Christian church has, consciously or unconsciously, colluded with a historical culture on the presumption that they shared the same vision, the message of the Cross and the Church's witness to it have invariably suffered.

A martyr-community, then, critically scrutinizes the times in which it must witness and carefully discerns how Christians must credibly live and die. Previous Christian generations in their respective cultures have never had the same type of moral dilemma that the nuclear armaments race, for example, raises up in our time. Among American Catholics, accustomed to strong military support of their government based on the principles of justified self-defense and a just war, the staggering moral implications of our current arms build-up may be obfuscated by a curious blend of Christian and cultural assumptions that have not been recently tested against the word of the Cross. The American bishops' willingness to struggle with an issue that could upset the complacency of many Catholics is but one example of the need for ongoing dialogue with and challenge to our cultural assumptions.

Yet even when the Christian community prophetically reassesses its position within a specific culture, its task is not finished. There is always the pressing need to deliver the message of the Cross in ways its contemporary culture can grasp and be challenged by. Cultures of any historical epoch tend to love the irrelevantly proclaimed Christian message since it disturbs nothing and quietly reinforces unexamined cultural values and goals. Whereas Augustine in his theological and pastoral thinking, for example, had to deal with the imminent cultural disintegration of the Roman empire due to the barbarian invasions, Thomas Aquinas and Bonaventure had to face the theological implications of an emerging urban society in the thirteenth century. Whether the pastoral praxis of the medieval church ever adequately came to grips with the need for a relevant translation of the theology of the Cross in that rapidly changing cultural situation is beyond the scope of this book. But it is worth noting that the initial effectiveness of the mendicant orders, like the Franciscans and Dominicans, was linked, in part, to their ability to translate the message of the Cross into the new cultural language of the thirteenth century.[63]

In an age such as ours, accustomed to rapid and sometimes unexamined cultural change, the need for martyr or witness communities of Christians is, perhaps, greater than ever before. Although the radical perspectives of the Cross may always be a "stumbling block" or "foolishness" to some, it would be ironic if the Christian community contributed to an irrelevant theology and praxis of the Cross. One way of avoiding this pitfall is to teach both the initiated and candidates how to keep measuring their culture against the Cross of Christ and its far-reaching implications.

Conclusions

The challenge of initiation begins with the Cross of Christ. The Christian community that lives and prays honestly is well aware of this. The argument of this first chapter can be summed up in this way: *the Cross of Christ accurately defines the Gospel values, vision, and praxis of the Christian community, and therefore, its theology and praxis of initiation.* Though Paul may not always directly link the Cross and the Church, these connections are implicit in the general development of his thought.[64] W. Klaiber echoes this conviction: "Paul understands the *'theologia crucis'* (the theology of the Cross) as having an ecclesial ring: not all are poor and despised, not all are persecuted and weak. But in solidarity with the weak and the suffering the community recognizes and maintains its place under the Cross."[65]

What can the contemporary churches learn from Paul's insistent "nothing but Jesus Christ and him crucified" (1 Cor. 2:2)?[66] First, we can relearn Paul's paradox that the only door to the resurrection is through the Cross. Second, this paradox is always difficult for the institutional church to live and to initiate others into. Our constant temptation is to reduce the mystery of God as revealed in the Cross to our own categories, and thus make mystery more "manageable." Paul counters this tendency with this emphasis on the mystery of God as revealed in the figure of the weak, crucified Lord who is strong with the power of God (2 Cor. 12:7–10).[67] As D. Lührmann has argued, with Paul revelation is no private preserve of elitist Christians, but "a new, committed, grace-filled activity of God that is linked to the Cross."[68]

The reader will notice that we have not discussed the early development of the passion narratives of the New Testament[69] nor the efforts of the pre-Pauline churches to clarify the redemptive meaning of Jesus' death on the Cross for them.[70] But the lesson to be learned from these earlier efforts of Christian communities is more pertinent than ever: the Christian community's willingness to live under the shadow of the Cross does affect the way she teaches both baptized and candidates to live the Gospel way and to pray as Jesus did.

The point of entry into the Christian community is the Cross. In a unique way, the Cross epitomizes the mystery of how God heals us and brings us together in Christ. The Cross marks the beginning of a long reassessment of what we prize in our lives, and why we do so. Above all, it is the Cross that tests the depth of our convictions and the width of our love. As we shall see, the lessons of the Cross accompany catechumens in their journey toward initiation. The impact of the Cross on the lives of both the candidates and the initiated is summed up in the admonition given the catechumen: "Receive the Cross on your forehead. . . . Learn how to know and follow him" (RICA, par. 83).

NOTES

1. See J. P. Meier, *The Vision of Matthew: Christ, Church and Morality in the First Gospel* (New York: Paulist, 1978), pp. 107–08, n. 105.
2. For the discussion of this "triple parallelism" in the structure of Matthew's gospel as well as scholarly opinions on the "stone of stumbling" background, see R. E. Brown, K. P. Donfried, J. Reumann, eds. *Peter in the New Testament* (New York: Paulist, 1973), pp. 93–95, and especially n. 218.
3. For a wider analysis of this pericope, see G. Bornkamm, "End-Expectation and Church in Matthew," G. Bornkamm, G. Barth, H. J. Held, eds. *Tradition and Interpretation in Matthew* (Philadelphia: Westminster, 1963), pp. 15–57; here, pp. 44–49.
4. Ibid., pp. 15–24.
5. Ibid., p. 48; see also, Meier, *The Vision of Matthew*, pp. 117–19.
6. This is not to say that Matthew is necessarily connecting chapters 16 and 26 in using this image of "stone of stumbling." See, for example, Brown, *Peter*, p. 94, n. 217; also, G. Stählin, *skandalon, Theological Dictionary of the New Testament* VII:348.
7. For Peter as the model leader and disciple, see Meier, *The Vision of Matthew*, p. 118, n. 120.
8. On the relation between Matt. 16 and John 21, see H. Thyen, *Studien zur Sündenvergebung im Neuen Testament und seinen alttestamentlichen und jüdischen Voraussetzungen* (Göttingen: Vandenhoeck & Ruprecht, 1970), pp. 236–59 passim.
9. Justin Matyr, *Apology*, I, 13, 4 as cited by M. Hengel, "Mors turpissima crucis: Die Kreuzigung in der antiken Welt und die 'Torheit' des 'Wortes vom Kreuz'," *Rechtfertigung: Festschrift E. Käsemann*, J. Friedrich, W. Pöhlmann, P, Stuhlmacher, eds. (Tübingen: J. C. B. Mohr, 1976), pp. 125–84; here, p. 126. See also, J. A. Fitzmyer, "Crucifixion in Ancient Palestine, Qumran Literature, and the New Testament," *Catholic Biblical Quarterly* 40 (1978):493–513.

10. See P. Stuhlmacher, "Achtzehn Thesen zur Paulinischen Kreuzestheologie," *Rechtfertigung* (supra. n. 9), pp. 509–25; here, p. 511.

11. Ibid.

12. K. Kertelge, "Das Verständnis des Todes Jesu bei Paulus," *Der Tod Jesu: Deutungen im Neuen Testament*, K. Kertelge, ed. (Herder: Freiburg, 1976), pp. 114–36; here, p. 120. For a somewhat different view, see G. Friedrich, *Die Verkündigung des Todes Jesu im Neuen Testament* (Neukirchen-Vluyn: Neukirchener, 1982), pp. 9–52.

13. E. Käsemann, "The Saving Significance of the Death of Jesus," *Perspectives on Paul* (Philadelphia: Fortress, 1971), pp. 32–59; here, p. 54; henceforth, *Perspectives*.

14. F. W. Gingrich, *Shorter Lexicon of the Greek New Testament* (Chicago: University of Chicago, 1965), p. 198; also, G. Stählin, *skandalon*, *Theological Dictionary of the New Testament* 7:339–58.

15. See W. Schmithals, *Gnosticism in Corinth*, J. E. Steely, trans. (Nashville: Abingdon, 1971); for an opposing position, see H. Conzelmann, *1. Corinthians* (Philadelphia: Fortress, 1975); henceforth, *1. Corinthians*.

16. E. Ellis has argued that verses 18–31 of 1 Corinthians are in the form of a Jewish homily, pivoting on the word-pattern: Wisdom (*sophia*)—scandal—wisdom; see his "Christ Crucified," *Prophecy and Hermeneutic in Early Christianity* (Grand Rapids: W. B. Eerdmans, 1978), pp. 72–79; here, p.72.

17. Conzelmann, *1. Corinthians*, pp. 43–44; U. Wilckens, *Weisheit und Torheit: Eine exegetisch-religionsgeschichtliche Untersuchung zu 1 Kor. 1 und 2* (Tübingen: J. C. B. Mohr, 1959), pp. 214–24; F-J. Ortkemper, *Das Kreuz in der Verkündigung des Apostels Paulus* (Stuttgart: Katholisches Bibelwerk, 1967), pp. 46–49.

18. P. Stuhlmacher, " 'Das Ende des Gesetzes.' Über Ursprung und Ansatz der paulinischen Theologie," *Zeitschrift für Theologie und Kirche* 67(1970):14–39; here, 35.

19. Phil. 2:6–11 has occasioned much scholarly writing. For summary of some of this scholarship, see G. Eicholz, *Die Theologie des Paulus im Umriss* (Neukirchen-Vluyn: Neukirchener, 1972), pp. 132–54; also, R. P. Martin, *Carmen Christi: Philippians ii. 5–11 in Recent Interpretation and in the Setting of Early Christian Worship* (Cambridge: University Press, 1967).

20. See, for example, G. Eicholz, *Paulus im Umriss*, p. 135; F. W. Beare, *A Commentary on the Epistle to the Philippians* (London: Adam & Charles, 1959), p. 85. It would be outside the scope and competence of this chapter to take a position on the exegetical debate about whether this is an "ethical example" to be applied to the Philippian community (compare Martin, *Carmen Christi*, pp. 214–16).

21. See G. Bornkamm, "On Understanding the Christ-Hymn (Philippians 2:6–11)," *Early Christian Experience* (New York; Harper & Row, 1969), pp. 112–22; here, p. 116.

22. I use the translation of R. Jewett, *Letter to Pilgrims: A Commentary on the Epistle to the Hebrews* (New York: Pilgrim, 1981), pp. 41–42; see also, ibid., pp. 44–45; F. F. Bruce, *The Epistle to the Hebrews* (Grand Rapids: W. B. Eerdmans, 1964), pp. 48–50; B. F. Westcott, *The Epistle to the Hebrews* (Grand Rapids: W. B. Eerdmans, 1974), p. 52, n. 14 for his comments on "participation."

23. See E. Käsemann, *Commentary on Romans* (Grand Rapids: W. B. Eerdmans, 1980), p. 157; henceforth, *Romans*.

24. Commenting on this verse, F. F. Bruce argues for translating the Greek as "Who has hypnotized you?" because "Their new behaviour was so strange, so completely at odds with the liberating message which they had previously accepted, that it appeared as if someone had put a spell on them"; see his *The Epistle to the Galatians: Commentary on the Greek Text* (Grand Rapids: W. B. Eerdmans, 1982), p. 148; henceforth, *Galatians*.

25. Friedrich, supra, n. 12, pp. 122–33.

26. Käsemann's commentary on this verse is to the point: "Incorporation into the rule of Christ and total separation from the law coincide" (*Romans*, p. 189). See also J. Moltmann, *The Crucified God* (New York: Harper & Row, 1974), p. 69.

27. See R. Duffy, *Real Presence: Worship, Sacraments and Commitment* (San Francisco: Harper & Row, 1982), pp. 32–57.

28. Bruce, *Galatians*, p. 271.

29. The Greek verb is *paradidometha*. See C. K. Barrett, *A Commentary on the Second Epistle to the Corinthians* (New York; Harper & Row, 1973), p. 140; henceforth, Barrett, *2 Corinthians*; also, W. Popkes, *Christus Traditus: Eine Untersuchung zum Begriff der Dahingabe im Neuen Testament* (Zürich: Zwingli, 1967), pp. 193–94.

30. See Käsemann's strong remarks on this point in *Perspectives*, pp. 37–38.

31. See F. W. Beare, *A Commentary on the Epistle to the Philippians* (London: A. & C. Black, 1959), p. 110.

32. Eichholz, *Paulus in Umriss*, p. 61.

33. For a discussion of this complex issue, see Barrett, *2 Corinthians*, pp. 5–10; B. Holmberg, *Paul and Power: The Structure of Authority in the Primitive Church as Reflected in the Pauline Epistles* (Philadelphia: Fortress, 1978), especially pp. 44–48.

34. Barrett, *2 Corinthians*, p. 336.

35. See R. C. Tannehill, *Dying and Rising with Christ* (Berlin: A. Töpelmann, 1967), pp. 14–20.

36. See J. Murphy-O'Connor, *Becoming Human Together: The Pastoral Anthropology of St. Paul* (Wilmington, Del.: M. Glazier, 1982), pp. 89–105; also, U. Wilckens, *Der Brief an die Römer (Röm. 1–5)* (Zürich: Benziger, 1978), pp. 307–14; A. Viard, *Saint Paul: Epître aux Romains* (Paris: Gabalda, 1975), pp. 136–37.

37. See M. Thrall, "Christ crucified or second Adam? A christological debate between Paul and the Corinthians," *Christ and Spirit in the New Testament*, B. Lindars, S. S. Smalley, eds. (Cambridge: University Press, 1973), pp. 143–56; especially p. 152.

38. Murphy-O'Connor, *Becoming Human Together*, p. 183.

39. Barrett, *A Commentary on the First Epistle to the Corinthians* (London: Adam Black, 1968), pp. 287–88; Conzelmann, *I Corinthians*, pp. 211–12.

40. Actually, the writer of Colossians speaks of "peace through the blood of the cross' (Col. 1:20) which some commentators find atypical in the Pauline corpus; see E. Schweizer, *The Letter to the Colossians* (Minneapolis: Augsburg, 1982), p. 84, n. 81; E. Lohse, *Colossians and Philemon* (Philadelphia: Fortress, 1971), pp. 43, 60 (n. 210); also, Friedrich, supra n. 12, pp. 108–10.

41. See B. Ahern, "The Christians' Union with the Body of Christ in Corinthians, Galatians, and Romans," *Catholic Biblical Quarterly* 23(1961):199–209. I owe this reference to J. Murphy-O'Connor's helpful suggestion.

42. Beare, *Philippians*, p. 72. G. Bertram, *phrēn*, *Theological Dictionary of the New Testament* 9:232–33; here, 233.

43. See J. P. Sampley, *Pauline Partnership in Christ* (Philadelphia: Fortress, 1980).

44. H. Conzelmann, *History of Primitive Christianity* (Nashville: Abingdon, 1973), pp. 108–09.

45. The American Bible translation (''united in love,'' *sunpsukhoi to hen phronountes*) might be literally translated ''together in soul considering the one thing.'' So, J. J. Muller, *The Epistles of Paul to the Philippians and to Philemon* (Grand Rapids: W. B. Eerdmans, 1955), p. 74, n. 8.

46. See, for example, R. Martin, *Philippians* (London: Oliphants, 1976), p. 88.

47. J. P. Sampley, *Pauline Partnership*, p. 67.

48. For similar uses of *phronein*, see 2 Cor. 13:11 and Rom. 12:16.

49. B. Lonergan, *Method in Theology* (New York: Herder and Herder, 1972), p. 79.

50. See E. Schüssler-Fiorenza, *Invitation to the Book of Revelation* (Garden City, N.Y.: Doubleday, 1981), pp. 56–57.

51. Ibid., for a more specific treatment of these problems, see pp. 61–67; J. M. Ford, *Revelation* (Garden City, N.Y.: Doubleday, 1975), pp. 386ff.

52. See J. Dunn, *Jesus and the Spirit* (Philadelphia: Westminster, 1975), pp. 173–74; E. Ellis, supra n. 16, pp. 28, 68, 224(n. 4).

53. ''Dogmatic Constitution on the Church (*Lumen Gentium*),'' Ch. 2, par. 17 (henceforth, ''The Church'') in *The Documents of Vatican II*, W. A. Abbott, ed. (New York: Guild Press, 1966), p. 36–7. (In future citations from the documents of Vatican II, the pagination from the Abbott edition will be given in parenthesis.)

54. P. Murnion, ''The Parish Community: Theological Questions,'' *Proceedings of the Catholic Theological Society of America* 36(1981):39–55; see also his *The Catholic Priest and the Changing Structure of Pastoral Ministry* (New York: Arno, 1978).

55. E. Schüssler-Fiorenza, *Priester für Gott: Studien zum Herrschafts- und Priestermotiv in der Apokalypse* (Münster: Aschendorff, 1972), pp. 263–90.

56. See R. Brown, ''New Testament Background for the Concept of the Local Church,'' *Proceedings of the Catholic Theological Society of America* 36(1981):1–14.

57. B. Lonergan, *Insight: A Study of Human Understanding* (New York: Harper & Row, 1978), p. 601; see also, R. M. Doran's discussion of the implications of Lonergan's idea in *Psychic Conversion and Theological Foundations: Toward a Reorientation of the Human Sciences* (Chico, Cal.: Scholars Press, 1981), pp. 101–04.

58. See M-L. Thérel, *Les Symboles de L' ''Ecclesia'' dans la Création iconographique de L'Art Chrétien du IIIᵉ au VIᵉ siècle* (Rome: Edizioni di Storia e Letteratura, 1973), pp. 125–33.

59. E. Leach, *Culture and Communication* (Cambridge: Cambridge University, 1976).

60. Conzelmann, *I Corinthians*, p. 112–113.

61. C. Geertz, *Interpretation of Cultures* (New York: Basic Books, 1973), p. 89.

62. See C. Molari, ''The Hermeneutical Role of the Christian Community on the Basis of Judaeo-Christian Experience,'' *Revelation and Experience, Concilium 113*, E. Schillebeeckx and B. van Iersel, eds. (New York: Seabury, 1979), pp. 93–105; here, p 96.

63. See P. Eicher, "Administered Revelation: The Official Church and Experience," *Revelation and Experience* (supra n. 62), pp. 3–17 for a complementary approach to the same problem.

64. Though, see W. Schrage, "Ist die Kirche das 'Abbild des Todes'?" *Kirche: Festschrift G. Bornkamm*, D. Lührmann and G. Strecker, eds. (Tübingen: J. C. B. Mohr, 1980), pp. 205–19.

65. W. Klaiber, *Rechtfertigung und Gemeinde: Eine Untersuchung zum paulinischen Kirchenverständnis* (Göttingen: Vandenhoecke & Ruprecht, 1982), p. 134; see also p. 137.

66. J. Moltmann, *The Crucified God* p. 28.

67. Again Barrett remarks that this image of Christ as weak and strong was "one basic form of New Testament Christology" (*2 Corinthians*, p. 336).

68. See the development of Paul's argument in 1 Cor. 2:1–8. D. Lührmann has argued very convincingly about the connections between revelation, "mystery," and the Cross in *Das Offenbarungsverständnis bei Paulus und in Paulinischen Gemeinden* (Neukirchen-Vluyn: Neukirchener, 1965), especially pp. 124–40. I will return to the implications of these connections in the last chapter.

69. For an excellent overview of the problems in this area, see J. R. Donahue, "Passion Narratives," *The Interpreter's Dictionary of the Bible*, Supplementary Volume (Nashville: Abingdon, 1976), pp. 643–45.

70. In addition to the bibliography already cited, see B. Lindars, "The Apocalyptic Myth and the Death of Christ," *Bulletin of the John Rylands Library* 57(1975):366–87; M. Hengel, "The Expiatory Sacrifice of Christ," *Bulletin of the John Rylands Library* 62(1980):454–75; J. Roloff, "Anfänge der soteriologischen Deutung des Todes Jesu," *New Testament Studies* 19(1972):38–64; J. P. Galvin, "Jesus' Approach to Death: An Examination of Some Recent Studies," *Theological Studies* 41(1980):713–44.

Chapter 2

A WORD THAT WILL
ROUSE THEM

The size of the average Sunday edition of any major newspaper would daunt even the most avid reader. Television and radio flood us with thousands of words daily. Computers are the most recent source of a potentially endless flow of sentences and paragraphs. But how many words can one read with attention, much less interest? When does the word become simply wordy, verbiage that no longer instructs or confronts?

Another challenge of initiation is the radical way in which God's Word transforms our words. In John's gospel, Jesus is presented as "the Word" (*logos*) enfleshed in human history. As we saw in the previous chapter, Paul can find no better measure of the Corinthians' commitment than the "word from the Cross" (1 Cor. 1:18). These are but two examples of how Scripture presents the Word of God as a synonym for his presence among his people. Invariably there is but one honest response to that Word—his people's words and actions that spring from a covenant commitment. In the last book of the New Testament, we saw one example of the link between God's Word and our response: "Let him who has ears heed the Spirit's word to the churches" (Rev. 2:7).

One way of summarizing the multilayered teaching of the word from the Cross is to see how it shapes Christians as a "church" whose mission is defined and enabled by that Cross. When the Church calls herself "the bride of the incarnate Word and the Pupil of the holy Spirit,''[1] she reminds herself of how she will be judged—faithfulness to the transforming praxis of God's Word. Paul, in fact, addresses such a test to the Corinthian church. The Greek text of his letter to them refers to their holding fast ''to the gospel as I gospeled it to you'' (1 Cor. 15:1).

When Vatican II reiterated the traditional teaching about the Word of God, however, it seemed almost like a new teaching to some Christians: ''He (Christ) is present in His word, since it is He himself who speaks when the Holy Scriptures are read in the church.''[2] This is the starting point for the honesty of the Church's response to God: his presence-filled Word which is at heart of all sacramental celebration, ecclesial mission, and shared commitment. Vatican II expressed this conviction in a practical liturgical rule: the celebration of the Word of God should normally precede any sacramental celebration.[3]

A Boring Word?

But does God's Word really transform the words, actions and vision of our lives? St. Cyril of Jerusalem, speaking to his catechumens in the fourth century, captures the perennial problem and continuing ideal of welcoming the Word of God: ''You were called a catechumen, that is, someone who heard hope and yet did not perceive it; who heard the mysteries, but did not understand them; who heard the scriptures but did not appreciate their depth. *Now you no longer hear only sounds, but you hear within.*''[4]

Although we have acquired sophisticated catechetical models and theologies about the Word of God, the rumor is abroad that the ''Word of God'' is boring the people of God. A constant pastoral complaint across this country is the way in which the Word of God is proclaimed and explained. As one theologian recently asked: ''is there any moment, in the . . . liturgy, or in any aspect of our church life and mission, less credibly theocentric than when the preacher preaches?''[5] Put another way, the theory and praxis of the Word of God seem to contradict one another too often in this post–Vatican II age. *Or worse, theory is mistaken for the praxis of the Word of God.* This should concern both theologians and the pastoral ministers of God's Word.

We usually answer this complaint with the familiar distinction drawn from sacramental theology: the objective nature of God's Word (*ex opere operato*) as opposed to the subjective reception and celebration of that Word (*ex opere operantis*). The distinction is a valid one when we honor the complementarity and balance between God's Word and our words in response. This distinction becomes a subterfuge at the moment when we forget how Isaiah describes the honest reception of God's Word: "The Lord God has given me a well-trained tongue that I might know how to speak to the weary a word that will rouse them. Morning after morning he opens my ear that I may hear; and I have not rebelled, have not turned back" (Isa. 50:4–5). But in too many celebrations across our country this assurance seems confounded by the boredom and apathy of both celebrants and participants of the liturgy of the Word. In the past, God's presence seemed to have evoked more than an occasional response from his listeners.

And yet, the response to God's Word was never measured by the rhetorical powers of the speaker. The writer of Luke–Acts seems to be describing a contemporary scene: "Paul talked on and on, and a certain young man named Eutychus who was setting on the window-sill became drowsier and drowsier" (Acts 20:9). But even after Eutychus has fallen from the third story to his death and Paul has restored him to life, the writer notes: "Then he talked for a long while—until his departure at dawn" (Acts 20:11). To the generations of boring preachers who have taken great consolation from this passage, it should be noted that the Word of God in Paul's mouth called forth communities of faith and evoked commitment to the Gospel. Our subject in this chapter, then, is not communications theory applied to the preaching of God's Word, valid as that discussion would be. Nor will effective preaching and teaching of God's Word be considered here, though it might sometimes seem to be in short supply.

God's presence-filled Word provides our unique assurance that we will be honest in our sacraments and the mission that Word calls us to. I acknowledge that God's Word-presence is a mystery not to be constrained by our constructs and theories. Therefore, even underneath apparent boredom and apathy, that same mystery of God's presence may be at work. *But that mystery is known in praxis, not in theory.* This is why we can believe at one and the same time that God's Word acts in hidden and unperceived ways in our shared and individual lives, and yet, that the Word cannot be so hidden that our self-serving definitions of conversion and mission are not constantly challenged.

I propose, then, to examine God's Word in a praxis situation, the catechumenal process. Liturgical catechesis and its words are rooted, after all, in God's Word. This is a unique context for hearing God's Word. The catechumenal process is always moving toward the commitments of initiation. When the Word of God is heard in such a context, it offers a praxis model for a knowing, active, and fruitful celebration and ministry of that Word.[6]

In discussing the Word of God as a formative element in becoming and remaining Christian, I am building on the work of others such as the hermeneutical insights of Hans-Georg Gadamer,[7] the semeiology of Roland Barthes and Roman Jakobson,[8] the seminal work of Paul Ricoeur on symbol,[9] Michael Polanyi's investigations into the meaning,[10] and Jürgen Habermas's continuing examination of praxis and communication.[11] Rather than rehearse this material, which is familiar to some readers and of too technical a nature to be of interest to others, I will turn immediately to the place of the Word of God in the catechumenal process and its implications for anyone who wishes to grow into a "new creation" in Christ.

The Table of God's Word

The manner in which a family welcomes someone into their midst either as a dinner guest or as a new member usually tells a great deal about that family. One of the key rituals of welcoming a candidate as a catechumen into the Church occurs at the moment of crossing the threshold of the church building. The celebrant in the name of the community says: "We welcome you into the church *to share with us at the table of God's word*" (RCIA, par. 90). The church community immediately follows through on this invitation by the celebration of God's Word in readings from Scripture and a homily. Then, in a ritual which is reminiscent of a similar gesture in a priest's ordination, the celebrant offers a copy of the Gospels to the catechumen with the words: "Receive the Gospel, the good news of Jesus Christ, the Son of God" (RCIA, par. 93).

But these words and actions will remain naive rituals if, as the RCIA notes, there has not first been a process of evangelization (par. 68). Evangelization comes from the Latin word for "gospel" and connotes a process of becoming familiar with and appropriating the values of the Kingdom of God. The celebrant's words to the catechumens prior to asking for some statement of commitment from them summarizes this process of evangelization: "Now the way of the Gospel opens before you, *inviting you to make a new beginning* by acknowledging the living God who speaks his words of truth to people. You are called to walk by the light of Christ and to trust in his wisdom: Are you ready to enter on this path today under the leadership of Christ?" (RCIA, par. 76).

The initial results of evangelization are symbolized in another ritual of this welcoming. Catechumens are, for the first time, marked with the sign of the cross by the celebrant, catechists, and sponsors with the striking words: "Receive the cross on your forehead: by this sign of his love Christ will be your strength. Learn now to know and follow him" (RCIA, par. 83). The ears, eyes, lips, breast, and shoulders are then similarly marked with the cross. As this is done, the celebrant prays that the catechumens might hear the voice of the Lord or respond to his Word (RCIA, par. 85).

The Cross and God's Word are interconnected. The first Christians in struggling with the meaning of Jesus' death began to hear God's Word in the psalms, the book of Isaiah, and so on, with new understanding. In oral and then written form, the New Testament was a response of commitment to the Cross and a challenge to whoever would listen. The power of the Cross enabled people, as St. Cyril would say, no longer to hear only the sounds of God's word, but to hear within themselves its meaning for their lives.

These rituals introduce a period, sometimes lasting several years (RCIA, par. 98), in which the Word of God will serve as a foundation for profound changes in the catechumen's life. The core experience of this time is the celebration of the Word of God. These celebrations should be a common table from which both the initiated and the candidates may be nourished (RCIA, par. 100). The Sunday celebration of the Eucharist, of course, has the liturgy of the Word as a permanent feature. But the catechumenal process implies a more frequence celebration. This is evident from the long-range goals that are envisaged in these celebrations of the Word.

The first of these goals is phrased in almost biblical language: "to implant in their hearts the teachings they are receiving" (RCIA, par. 106a). In other words, the catechumenal or conversion process cannot be reduced to an intellectual preparation, though Christianity has always enjoyed a rich theological tradition. The RCIA illustrates what is meant by "teaching" in the unique New Testament approach to responsible Christian living. As noted in Chapter 1, this New Testament morality is not a Christianized stoicism, but rather a view of life and its purposes that has been shaped by the message of the Cross and verified by the resurrection.

A second result of celebrating God's Word is learning how to pray. There were periods in the history of the Church in which Christian prayer seemed to have been presented as an experience independent of God's Word. And yet, the prayers of Jesus, the blessings of Mary and Zachary, and the vibrant Pauline words of praise to God continue the rich Old Testament tradition of acknowledging God's presence. Because God's Word continues to reveal our need and his compassion, prayer becomes a natural accompaniment to Scripture, much like the musical setting of an insightful text. The liturgical celebration of God's Word by the whole community, with its accompanying prayer, has always been seen as both a model of and and invitation to prayer.

Finally, the RCIA sees the Word of God as the teacher of good liturgy and a door to its symbols, seasons, and meanings. Liturgy is the shared and grateful response of the Christian community to the continuing and healing mystery of God's presence among us. For two thousand years, that Word has been a formative element in becoming Christian. But it is not difficult to demonstrate that each time liturgy has become impoverished in its celebration of the Word of God, not as ritual but as presence, there has been a loss of meaning and challenge in the general worship of the Church.

These goals, however, seem more like theory than reality in some Christian communities. Of what use is it to form candidates in this dynamic understanding of God's Word when many of the baptized do not seem to be influenced by an extended experience with "liturgies of the Word"? In the post–Vatican II church, when the Sunday liturgy of the Word, for example, with its three scriptural readings, responsorial psalm, and a homily may be finished in twenty minutes, are we pastorally realistic about the goals of conversion, prayer, and honest worship?

The proper context for answering such questions is the type of Christian community that celebrates such a liturgy of the Word. Chapter 1 proposed the model of a Christian community that takes the message of the Cross and its implications seriously. We have already suggested that the New Testament, in a very real sense, is a response to the meaning of the Cross, and that the Old Testament was seen in a new light because of that same Cross. When the RCIA proposes the process by which someone becomes committed to Christ, a measure is set before those who regard themselves as already Christian, both as a community and individually. The way in which the Word of God reshapes our vision of his world is one necessary measure of being Christian. The concerns of this chapter, then, focus on the community that gives the Gospels to the candidates and on the catechumens who hear it. If Christian communities resist the measure of God's Word, then Leonard Bernstein's troubling text in *Mass* may be true of them: "So we wait in silent treason until reason is restored, And we wait for the season of the Word of the Lord."[12]

The Ancient Catechumenal Process

To understand the importance of the Word of God both in renewing the Christian community and in forming individuals as Christians, we must take a brief look at the praxis of the process in earlier centuries. While we cannot hope to reconstruct a detailed picture of how the Word of God shaped the catechumenal process from the passing allusions of a Tertullian or an Origen, we can certainly note some general characteristics that will help our discussion. Over fifty years ago, G. Bardy and Dom B. Capelle, in their classic studies of the origins of the catechumenate, offered a starting point.

Bardy argued that the precursors of the catechumenate at Rome were schools conducted by converted philosophers such as St. Justin Martyr. These schools were not directly under the leadership of the

Christian communities at Rome. Only with the heretical turn of some of these teachers did the local church assume preparation of all candidates for initiation.[13] Bardy describes Justin Martyr's method as comparable to that of other pagan teachers. In a series of questions and answers, he would deal with the Word of God and its diverse interpretations, adjusting his style to the different backgrounds of Jews or pagans. But, unlike other pagan schools at Rome, this teaching was a witness to the "Good News" and an invitation to a change of life-style and values. Justin as a martyr summarized the unique characteristic of this teaching of the Word of God at its best—a radical life-praxis rooted in the Gospel.

Dom B. Capelle, in analyzing this same period at Rome, notes that the Greek mystery religions had their own ritual catechumenate. He then cites Origen: "The profound and secret mysteries must not be given, at first, to disciples, but they must be first instructed in the correction of their life-styles."[14] Capelle then adds Origen's response to Celsus, the second-century pagan philosopher: "When it becomes evident that the disciples *are purified by the word and have begun, as far as possible, to live better*, only then are they invited to know our mysteries."[15]

One major characteristic of the catechumenal process begins to emerge: God's Word leads to commitments long before it leads to initiation. These commitments were shaped, in part, by the tenor of the times such as intermittent persecutions, the continuing need for witness in a hostile environment, and the mutual expectations of christians united in communities of faith. Thus, the well-known debate about when the catechumenate was institutionalized sometimes misses the crucial point.[16] "Baptism without delay" did not imply less commitment but less time to evoke the commitment. The catechumen of today might well be the martyr of tomorrow.

On the other hand, three years "hearing the word" in the catechumenate of Hippolytus at Rome in the early third century might seem long until we reflect on the quality of commitment that was expected of any Christian at the time.[17] Hippolytus tells us that the first time inquirers came "in order to hear the word" (*ad audiendum verbum*), the teachers questioned them on their motivation, their life situation, and their willingness to change work that might hinder the practice of God's Word.[18] As Origen, another third-century theologian, summarily states it: "You must upon hearing the Word of God, root out your habitual vices and allay your barbaric customs so that . . . you will be able to receive the Holy Spirit."[19]

A second characteristic has recently been suggested, that the catechumenal process sought to share the affections.[20] In other words, nonintellectual dimensions of a candidate's response were considered an important area of conversion. The reception of Christian teaching in Cyril of Jerusalem's thought, for example, is conditioned by the affective state of the candidate. Conversion touches every area of the human story. If God's Word is to grasp us, then heart as well as mind must be opened to its message. We will return to this point later in this chapter.

Tertullian, a third-century North African theologian, who seems to have had firsthand experience in dealing with the catechumens, describes their first hearing of the Word of God: "it (penitence) presses most urgently, however, upon those recruits who have just begun to give ear to the flow of divine discourse, and who, like puppies newly born, creep about uncertainly, with eyes as yet unopened." He continues, "Let no one flatter himself, therefore, that because he is classed among the auditors in the catechumenate, he is, on that account, still permitted to sin. . . . We are not baptized so that we may cease committing sin but because we have ceased. . . . This, surely, is the first Baptism of the catechumen."[21]

In brief, the catechumenal process invites people to hear and see reality with God's ears and eyes. The biblical image of conversion as a "walk" captures the change in such listeners to God's Word. They should walk in a new way, having heard God's message and seen his Future, the Kingdom.

The Emmaus Walk

To illustrate the theology of the Word of God behind the catechumenal process both in the post–Vatican II church and in the early Christian church, we turn to a famous "walk" in the New Testament. In Luke's gospel, one of the most compelling of the postresurrection stories is the journey of two disciples from Jerusalem to Emmaus (Luke 24:13–35). As Hans Dieter Betz has suggested, this carefully modulated story traces the origin of Christian faith in the person.[22] The resurrected Jesus who walks with the two confused disciples "is present in the living word-event as it happens in discussion and proclamation of various kinds."[23]

Jesus approaches the two disciples as they are reviewing all that has happened in the previous week. Jesus, unrecognized as yet, inquires about the subject of their "lively exchange," as Luke describes it (Luke 24:15). Their answer is a summary of who Jesus was in their minds: "a prophet powerful in word and deed," and "one who would set Israel free" (Luke 24:19,21). As Betz observes, they know the facts, but do not understand their meaning for them.[24] Their christology cannot seem to support a crucified Lord. Once again, the Cross is experienced as a "stone of stumbling." Jesus' questions have probed the unreflected religious experience of these two disciples and uncovered the obstacles to their welcoming the unexpected process of salvation.

The Cross of Christ has overturned the expectations of these disciples. We touch the heart of the matter. Luke presents the story because years after the event Calvary is still a troubling enigma for people who try to believe. Prospective disciples suspect (and correctly so) that if salvation is through the Cross, then their own ideas on the "good life" will have to change. This "walk"—the biblical metaphor for conversion, as we noted above—is a study in how the Word of God prepares us for the Word from the Cross: "Beginning, then, with Moses and all the prophets, he interpreted for them every passage of scripture which referred to him" (Luke 24:27).[25] The Word of God is Jesus' proof that the Messiah had to endure his suffering "so as to enter into his glory" Luke 24:26).

The familiar ending of the story includes not only the belated recognition by the disciples of Jesus in the breaking of the bread at table, but in the admission, "Were not our hearts burning inside us as he talked to us on the road and explained the Scriptures to us?" (Luke 24:32). The Word of God in Jesus' mouth had not only been source of intellectual insight, but a total experience for these two disciples. Luke's proof of this change in them is simple. The disciples return to the city they had just fled. In response to the news of Christ's resurrection from those who remained at Jerusalem, "they recounted what had happened on the road and how they had come to know him in the breaking of the bread'' (Luke 24:35). The scholarly debate about whether Luke is describing a eucharistic meal need not concern us here.[26] The underlying theme of progressive growth in faith, however, is of major importance to those who would welcome God's Word.

It hardly seems accidental that there are two other stories in the Lucan writings that contain striking similarities with the Emmaus story. In the same chapter, Luke reports Jesus' final appearance to the Eleven (Luke 24:36–49) with the same sequence of themes that we saw earlier in the chapter: a recollection of how Jesus fulfills the message of the Scriptures, the necessity of his suffering, his resurrection, and the ensuing insight of the disciples.[27] A similar account in the Acts of the Apostles tells how Philip and the eunuch of the Ethiopian queen meet while traveling. Once again, there is a question of understanding the Scriptures (in this case, the book of Isaiah) and the suffering of Jesus (the references to the suffering servant in Isaiah 53). Philip's explanation leads to the eunuch's baptism (compare the disciples' breaking of bread at Emmaus) and the resulting joy.[28] Prescinding from the technical questions of how these stories are related, the delineation of the step-by-step growth in awareness and faith remains a guide for us.

Doing the Emmaus Walk

The context for the proclamation of the Word of God is the Christian community that sees its own experience reflected in the Scriptures as announced and believed. As R. Schreiter argues, God's revelation, as an ongoing communicative activity, also allows the community to specify and interpret anew its current as well as its past experience.[29] In the process of initiation, the Christian community invites candidates to begin the ''walk'' that will continue to the moment of death. We do not exhaust the meaning of the Cross or the resurrection with our simple categories and creeds. The Risen Lord constantly teaches the Church to ''see'' the redemptive meanings of these events within the contexts of its past and current experience. For it is the shallow readings of our experience that sometimes allow us to stumble rather than ''walk'' as Christians. The scandal of the Cross can once again loom large when our communal or personal experience seems devoid of meaning. Economic privation in a country or neighborhood, a senseless killing, a violent rape, or an unexpected terminal illness in an individual's life are but a few examples of experience in search of Christian meaning. The Cross has never ceased to be the first step in any such search.

True to the Emmaus description, this relearning process always begins with our disruptive life-experience and our too tidy formulas about God's action and power in our lives. Most people, baptized or not, have some idea about "what the Bible says." But this is not yet the Emmaus experience. The two disciples in Luke's account, in fact, use their misunderstanding of God's purpose to argue implicitly that the Cross should not have happened. "Prophet" and "freedom" in their mouth (compare Luke 24:19,21) mean something radically different than the explanation this "stranger" offers.

And so, we move from our misunderstanding of our story and God's words to the disclosing event of God's Word. In the various Lucan stories that seem to follow this Emmaus model, the familiar texts of Scripture are torn open to reveal God's presence, which is his meaning. After all, new knowledge of God in itself would change nothing. *But Jesus' disclosure of God's action in the events of the Cross is an enabling event.* The biblical account of the disciples' reaction to Jesus' disclosure ("our hearts burning inside us") does not refer to an emotional "high," but to a moment of decision and change. When the meaning is disclosed, the listener must still choose to welcome the power and healing of that experience, as did the two Emmaus disciplines.

This disclosing and enabling power of God's Word remains the starting point for the journey toward his Kingdom. The Word of God is the bridge between his purposeful action in our world and our communal and individual struggle for meaning in that same world. The Word of God in the catechumenal process and in the celebration of the sacraments are but two examples of how the Church invites us to "walk" again with the Risen Lord and to make his meanings our own. The resulting insight is no barren intellectual idea, but rather a decisive moment or period of our lives. The choice we make will be seen in the ways we praise God and proclaim his resurrection with new conviction and commitment.[30]

The results of welcoming God's Word are captured in the "recognition" scene that concludes the Emmaus story. As already noted, the scholarly debate over the eucharistic context of Jesus and the disciples at table should not distract us from the importance of this "recognition." In Scripture, recognition scenes always seem to accompany a new awareness of God's action in people's lives. The Latin root of "recognition" means "to know again." In the dynamic biblical idea, to believe is to know God again and again within the changing contexts of our shared experience. Luke reminds us that God's living Word continues to invite us to this experience and the renewed praise of God that inevitably follows.

Word of God as Praxis-Event

The catechumenal process is an experience of Christian praxis in which the Emmaus "walk" is constantly experienced as an event that discloses and contrasts our own and God's vision of reality. In the catechumenal process as in the Emmaus scene, *the Word of God is a praxis-event that uncovers the praxis or "doings" of our lives*. G. Bornkamm states it this way: "God's word has become one with the simplest human word. . . . For Paul, God's word is the word that he can declare only in the reality of his own humanity."[31] After all, what God does in justification cannot be separated from his presence-filled Word. Neither the radical purposelessness that God rescues us from, nor the surprising future he calls us to can be appreciated or accepted from a theoretical position. Rather, God's Word starts with our self-serving narratives that provide the excuses for not taking his message seriously.

When Augustine, for example, seems to hear the child's sing-song "Take up and read," he is still struggling with the cost of conversion. It is not intellectual doubt, but rather the praxis of his life that is an obstacle to welcoming the Gospel. Yet at that moment in the garden, he is finally ready to bring the contexts of his life to the familiar texts of God's Word. He is ready to "take up and read." Augustine's reactions still stirs us: "So I hurried back to the place where Alpius was sitting, for when I stood up to move away, I had put down the book containing Paul's Epistles. I seized it and opened it, and in silence I read the first passage on which my eyes fell: 'Not in reveling and drunkenness, not in lust and wantonness, not in quarrels and rivalries. Rather, arm yourself with the Lord Jesus Christ, spend no more thought on nature or nature's appetites.' I had no wish to read more and no need to do so. For in an instant, as I came to the end of the sentence, it was as though the light of confidence flooded into my heart and all darkness of doubt was dispelled.''[32]

The catechumenal process, at its most effective, has always enabled the hearer to contextualize his or her antecedent experience of God through the Word of God. The texts of God's Word bring the familiar contours of our own autobiographical narrative into a new perspective in which we see that God loved us before we loved him. In other words, the Word of God, honestly attended to, inevitably reveals God's continuing justifying power in our lives. This is never simply a theoretical insight, but rather a praxis situation that is revelatory. It is again the Emmaus experience with ''hearts burning within'' and recognition of the hitherto unrecognized Lord. We will return to this idea in chapter 3.

Earlier in this chapter, we alluded to the frequent complaint that the Word of God as celebrated, preached, and taught sometimes seems to have nothing to do with the dynamic experience of the walk to Emmaus. The ministries of the Church should be an aid, not an obstacle to Christians as they attempt to ''take up and read'' God's Word. We must turn, then, to the pastoral implementation of this theology of the Word of God.

The Season of the Word of the Lord

''And we wait for the season of the Word of the Lord''—Leonard Bernstein's text, cited earlier, hints at the problem of proclaiming and welcoming God's Word. For some people, waiting is synonymous with delaying or even avoiding the impact of God's Word. For others, waiting is a dynamic time and space between their current lives and God's future. The Word of God teaches us how to deal with that in-between time. A practical question immediately emerges when we make such statements. Are the ministries which purport to help us hear God's Word effective? Do these ministries help us enter into the Emmaus experience in our own time?

Many Christians are involved in the ministry of God's Word— preachers, teachers, parents, catechumenal personnel, lectors, and so forth. Not surprisingly, it is the Word of God that teaches these ministers how they should assist others to welcome that same Word. After all, where would Timothy be without the help of Paul, or Augustine without the preaching of Ambrose? When the ministry of the Word of God has proved helpful to others, it could not be confused with a mere recitation of theological statements, with moral harangues, or with professional rhetoric.

Paul once again gives us the measure of the ministry of the Word: "Our preaching of the gospel proved *not a mere matter of words for* you but one of power; it was carried on in the Holy Spirit, and out of complete conviction" (1 Thess. 1:5). In contrast to the words of the "wise," Paul reaches back to the Old Testament notion of the enabling and fruitful Word of God that can accomplish all things.[33] This is the Word he proclaimed to the Thessalonians. A second characteristic of the Pauline ministry of the Word is his conviction.[34] The gospel has continued to motivate and transform his life. Paul, therefore, preaches from his experience of God's healing Word.

No minister of God's Word is given anything less than Paul to preach—the same enlivening Word. Like Paul, every person who offers God's Word to others can find in their own experience what God has done for them. It is this recognition that is the ground for the convinced ministry of the Word. At least some of the current complaints about the boring irrelevancy of some preaching and teaching can be traced to the attitudes of the ministers of God's Word. This is not to question the objective dimension of God's presence in his Word, but to say that the ministers of that Word also have responsibilities based on his action in their lives. A convinced witness is a necessary component of the proclamation of God's Word. Otherwise, computers might well substitute for a mindless or uncommitted recitation of the words of God.

This is the thrust of Paul's reminder to his hearers: "we wanted to share with you not only God's tidings but our very lives" (1

Thess. 2:8).[35] The result of this type of preaching is imitation. Much has been written on the biblical notion of imitation in which God or Jesus serves as a pattern for one's life. After recalling how the Thessalonians became imitators of himself, Paul notes proudly how they, in turn, have become a model for other Christians in Macadonia and Achaia (1 Thess. 1:6–7).[36] Imitation is, in effect, a living out of the self-gift of Jesus in such a way that we become a model for other communities of Christians.[37]

Those who preach, teach, and proclaim the Scriptures in the liturgical assembly should be examples of how "to wait for the season of the Lord" by the ways in which they struggle honestly to allow the texts of God's Word to bring them back to the contexts of their own lives. This honesty does not demand autobiographical references in one's preaching or teaching, but rather a renewed awareness that the experience of the Emmaus disciples has also been ours on more than one occasion.

The Word of God and Mission

There is no further mention of the Emmaus disciples in the gospel of Luke after their return to Jerusalem. One certain thing, however, is that Jesus did not open up the meaning of the Scriptures for their private consolation. The Emmaus disciples were given the Word to share with others. *There is no fruitful celebration of the Word of God that does not ultimately lead to more committed participation in the mission of the Risen Lord.* This connection between the Word of God and mission is especially prominent in the catechumenal process. The catechumen may not idly list to the Word of God. Even before the official catechumenate begins, evangelization, as proclamation of the living God,[38] prepares the way for discipleship. The RCIA states clearly that the Word of God is celebrated with catechumens so that Christ's teaching may be implanted in their hearts, not simply in their minds.[39]

But how does this happen in praxis? We always hear the Word of God within a certain situation. As W. Kasper has pointed out, the Word in a particular situation or context assumes its full force and precise focus.[40] Going a step further, I would suggest it is the very nature of the dynamic Word of God that the familiar praxis-situation of our lives is perceived in new ways. Our intentionality shaped by our unevangelized views and goals continues to focus on and react to our life-situations in unchristian ways (a point we will develop in chapter 3). For better or worse, we frame our situations with meaning. But God's Word contests the ways in which we hear and see our reality. God's Word challenges the self-serving purposes of our lives.

Mission is based on God's view of reality. No one can be in mission because they have read a book about it. Rather, they are sent who have first heard and seen. As the writer of 1 John points out, proclamation stems from experience: "what we have heard, what we have seen with our eyes, what we have looked upon and our hands have touched—we speak of the word of life" (1 John 1:1)[41] Only when God's vision of a new creation has been glimpsed, can we participate in announcing that vision. Without that same Word of God accompanying us on our mission, we would forget why we had set out in the first place, and the vision that inspired us.[42] When we have encountered the presence-filled Word of God once again and we are asked, "Whom shall I send? Who will go for us?" we, like Isaiah, can have a ready answer: "Here am I. Send me" (Isa. 6:8).

On a praxis level, why do so many good people hear the Word of God and yet seem to do little but guard a private piety? Perhaps Paul VI put his finger on the problem: "Those who sincerely accept the Good News, through the power of this acceptance and of shared faith, therefore, gather together in Jesus' name in order to seek together the kingdom, build it up and live it. They make up a community which is in its turn evangelizing."[43] In effect, Paul VI follows the Pauline chain-syllogism of Romans 10; calling on the name of the Lord presumes belief. But belief assumes hearing the Word of God, which, in turn, entails preaching. The source of all preaching, however, is mission (Rom. 10:13–15).[44] Such mission in Pauline theology is rooted in the Christian community.

I suspect that there are contemporary communities who believe that they can be Christian without mission. In such communities, the Word of God does not bear fruit because the Word becomes privatized and and moralized. The parable of the sower does not disquiet the complacency of such communities because they think that they know the meaning of Jesus' warning, and they do not. The parable foretells the eschatological success of God's Word.[45] But the realistic description of those who hear with joy and yet fall away remains (Luke 8:12–14).

The local church, therefore, has the same responsibility toward the baptized but unevangelized Christians as she does toward the catechumens: to provide a focus for the mission that the Word of God evokes in her midst. If catechumenal candidates for confirmation, for example, impelled by the living Word of God, look around their world and ask what it means to "be sent," the local church should be able to help them answer this question in a contextualized and appropriate way.

The Young Christian Worker movement, earlier in this century, provides an example of enabling young people to take the Word of God seriously. Young workers, many of who had little formal education, were invited to hear and pray over the Word of God so as to be able to decide and act on its meaning for their lives. This process was at the heart of the movement that attracted large numbers of young adults who had been considered lost to the Church.

Words of Praise

Another corollary that flows from an honest praxis of the Word of God is this: *the Word of God puts honest praise on the lips of Christians.* In the catechumenal process, people learn to praise God as a result of the revealing Word of God. As R. Schreiter has pointed out, the New Testament, for example specified in multiple ways the experience of Jesus. But this process always ends in confession and praise.[46] Liturgy, in turn, provides the same specification process by which the Christian community moves past the labels of praise to the experience of unearned salvation which must be voiced.

But how does the Word of God do this? In the catechumenal process, the Word of God contests the choices and priorities that summarize our lives. There are no theories here. The Word of God presents radically different choices and priorities: "Indeed, God's word is living and effective, sharper than any two-edged sword. It penetrates and divides soul and spirit, joints and marrow; it judges the reflections and thoughts of the heart'' (Heb. 4:12). Because God's Word reveals our redemptive need, it discloses the ground of our praise.[47] Because God's Word shows the void in which we have been and from which we continue to be rescued, it prods our dull tongues to praise the gracious gift of God's love.

When Augustine, for example, discusses the power of the sacraments, he must review what the honest Christian brings to event. After posing the question about where the water of baptism derives its power from, he answers: ''By the action of the word, not because it is said, but because it is believed.''[48] Although Augustine is speaking here of the words accompanying the sacramental action of baptism, his thought is equally applicable to the way in which the Word of God prepares us for honest and fruitful participation in every sacramental and worship experience. The language of the Word of God is heuristic in that it pushes us past our own boundaries of meaning, and thus, helps us to symbolize praise with God's larger meanings. God's Word, like sacraments, includes prescriptive language in the deepest sense of the word. We learn the obedience of faith and our words of praise reflect that faith.[49]

His Word and Our Hope

And so, we return to Bernstein's line: ''We wait for the season of the Word of the Lord.'' The ways in which we wait are shaped by our vision of the future. Put another way, our hope defines the way we currently live. Our implicit argument throughout this chapter has been that *the Word of God shapes our eschatological hope*. A historical example might illustrate this statement. Christian communities at Rome or in North Africa in the third century had the practical pastoral problem of catechumens being scandalized by the lapse of the baptized under torture and persecution. The remarkable fact is that so many catechumens did not become cynical, but witnessed their hope in the Kingdom of God, even to the death. I suspect that the same Word of God that strengthened weak Christians to witness eventually to the Gospel enabled catechumens to hope in the promises of God.

Paul argues that Jesus' obedience is the source of our eschatological hope: ''Jesus was never anything but 'Yes.' Whatever promises

God has made have been fulfilled in him; therefore, it is through him that we address our Amen to God when we worship together. God is the one who firmly establishes us along with you in Christ. It is he who has anointed us and has sealed us, therefore depositing the first payment, the Spirit, in our hearts'' (2 Cor. 1:19–22).[50]

The Kingdom of God defines what Christ accomplished and what we are called to. There is no hope within the Church that does not look toward that Kingdom. When respectable cynicism and liturgical disbelief prosper in Christian communities, then one must ask what has happened to the Word of God. Are we waiting for the season of the Word of the Lord?

"Waiting," of course, is an eschatological stance. It is the way in which we welcome God's future. But there is no Christian waiting worth the name that is not grounded in a profound hope in God's promises. Because the Word of God stretches the meanings that make sense of our life and work, hope becomes a vision that is renewed many times in the life of each Christian. Just as the parables of Christ must teach us our ignorance of God's Kingdom so that we might learn to welcome it, so, paradoxically, the jagged contours of our life-experience push us to the frontiers of God's meaning and the source of our hope, the Kingdom.

In psychological language, we say that a person anticipates events by figuring our similar experiences.[51] Expressed differently, we are always in the process of learning how to hope. We have argued, however, that our vision of the future helps define our current hopes. Such religious hope is never a private affair, but enables us, as Lonergan insists, "to resist the vast pressures of social decay." [52] To wait for the season of the Word of the Lord is, then, to wait in a shared hope that builds up a Christian community of shared meaning. Such communities can always witness in flawed but credible ways to the truth of God's Word in their own time.

Some Conclusions

No Christian community is excused from proclaiming the Word of God with conviction and credibility. This assertion is not based on the rhetorical or theological skills of the ministers of God's Word nor on their personal merits. Paul definitively reminded the Church that God is always healing and enabling us, long before we have theories about his presence and action in our lives. We proclaim and we hear the Word of God within the very context that he alone can provide: his presence engraved in the stories of our lives.

No Christian is offered less than the experience of the Lord given to perplexed disciples on their way to Emmaus. Luke seems to remind the Church in this account that the Word of the Risen Lord always brings Christians back to the meaning of the Crucified Lord and its implications for our future journeys in time. The Word of God starts with our flawed and misunderstood life-situations. Once again, we are invited to discover the deeper meanings that have eluded us. Recognition of the Lord at our table will cost both the baptized and the catechumens the same effort to listen more attentively to the Word and to invite more warmly its author, the teaching Lord, to continue on the journey with them.

There are some pastoral corollaries to this theological understanding of the Word of God. Too much preaching and teaching seems to address the people of God as if he had not continually touched the experience of their lives. The result is declarative theological sentences that neither challenge nor clarify that experience. There is a subtle arrogance in such mindless recitation of salvation history.

Second, one suspects that there are still too many catechumenal programs that are disguised forms of the old convert instruction programs of the forties. The problem with these programs was not the objective teaching of the Church, but rather the lack of a vital connection between the meaning of people's experience and that teaching. Augustine expressed that necessary dynamic link with great perception: "Indeed where our thinking attains what we know and is therein formed, then our word is true."[53]

As so, "I wait, you wait, we wait," for the season of the Word of the Lord. Together we conjugate the experience of God's Word transforming our words. "Then someone said to me: 'Do not seal up the prophetic words of this book, for the appointed time is near! . . . The One who gives testimony says, 'Yes, I am coming soon.' Amen! Come, Lord Jesus!'' (Rev. 22:10,20). At that moment, our words and God's Word will be one.

NOTES

1. "Dogmatic Constitution on Divine Revelation (*Dei Verbum*)," par. 23 Supra chap. 1, n. 53 (p. 126).
2. "Constitution on the Sacred Liturgy (*Sacrosanctum Concilium*)," par. 7 supra chap. 1, n. 53 (p. 141).
3. Ibid., par. 24 (p. 147); par. 35 (pp. 149–50); par. 56 (pp. 156–57).
4. *The Protocatechesis*, 6. I have translated freely from the revised Greek text of F. L. Cross, *St. Cyril of Jerusalem's Lectures on the Christian Sacraments* (Crestwood, N.Y.: St. Vladimir's Seminary Press, 1977), p. 4.
5. A. Lewis, "Ecclesia ex auditu: A Reformed View of the Church as the Community of the Word of God," *Scottish Journal of Theology* 35(1982):13–31; here, 14.
6. "Constitution on the Sacred Liturgy," par. 11 (p. 143).
7. H-G. Gadamer, *Truth and Method* (New York: Seabury, 1975), especially pp. 366–477.
8. R. Barthes, *Le Degré zéro de L'Ecriture* (Paris: Gonthier, 1964); also his *Essais Critiques* (Paris: Seuil, 1964). R. Jakobson, *Essais de Linguistique Générale* (Paris: Minuit, 1963).
9. I would especially cite P. Ricoeur's "Structure, Word, Event," in *The Conflict of Interpretations*, D. Ihde, ed. (Evanston: Northwestern University, 1974), pp. 79–96; idem, *Interpretation Theory: Discourse and the Surplus of Meaning* (Fort Worth, Texas: Texas Christian University, 1976); idem, "Biblical Hermeneutics," *Semeia* 4(1975):29–148; also, J. Van Den Hengel, *The Home of Meaning: The Hermeneutics of the Subject of Paul Ricoeur* (Washington, D.C.: University Press of America, 1982).
10. M. Polanyi, *The Tacit Dimension* (New York: Doubleday, 1966); M. Polanyi and H. Prosch, *Meaning* (Chicago: University of Chicago, 1975); also, J. Apczynski, *Doers of the Word* (Missoula, Montana: Scholars Press, 1977).
11. Habermas's most useful works for our concerns are *Theory and Practice* (Boston: Beacon, 1974); also, T. McCarthy, *The Critical Theory of Jürgen Habermas* (Cambridge, Mass.: MIT Press, 1978).
12. L. Bernstein, *Mass: A Theatre Piece for Singers, Players, and Dancers* (New York: G. Schirmer, n.d.), p. 12.
13. G. Bardy, "Les Ecoles Romaines au Second Siècle," *Revue d'histoire ecclésiastique* 28(1932):501–32.
14. D. Capelle, "L'Introduction du catéchuménat à Rome," *Recherches de théologie ancienne et médiévale* 5(1933):129–54; the Origen reference is to Hom. V, 6 in Iud. (ibid. p. 151, n. 38).
15. C. Cels. 3, 59, as cited by Capelle, ibid., p. 151, n. 39 (italics mine).
16. See A. Turck, "Aux Origines du Catéchuménat," *Revue des Sciences Philosophiques et Théologiques* 48(1964):20–31.
17. *The Apostolic Tradition of Hippolytus*, par. 17; in the critical edition of B. Botte, *La Tradition Apostolique de Saint Hippolyte* (Münster: Aschendorff, 1963), p. 39.
18. Ibid., par. 15–16; Botte ed., pp. 33, 34–35. See also, A. Turck, "Catéchein et Catéchesis chez les premiers Pères," *Revue de Sciences Philosophiques et Théologiques* 47(1963):361–72; here, 363. The "two ways" of the *Didaché*

can be analyzed, in a similar way, as an evangelical commitment teaching that was to lead to initiation. For the critical text, see J-P. Audet, *La Didaché: Instruction des Apôtres* (Paris: Gabalda, 1958), pp. 226–33. In addition to Audet's remarks (ibid., pp. 263–64), see J. Daniélou, *The Theology of Jewish Christianity* (Chicago: H. Regnery, 1964), pp. 316–21.

19. Hom. in Luc. 21, 4, as cited by M. Dujarier, *A History of the Catechumenate* (New York: Sadlier, 1979), p. 33.

20. J. Berntsen, "Christian Affections and the Catechumenate," *Worship* 52(1978):194–210.

21. Tertullian, "On Penitence," *Treatises on Penance*, translated by W. LeSaint (Westminster, Md.: Newman, 1959), pp. 24, 25–26.

22. H. Betz, "The Origin and Nature of Christian Faith," *Interpretation* 23(1969):32–46; here, 38–39. For a different position on this text, see I. H. Marshall, *The Gospel of Luke* (Grand Rapids: W. B. Eerdmans, 1978), pp. 889–900. For a critical background of the text, see ibid., pp. 890–91 and J-M. Guillaume, *Luc interprète des anciennes traditions sur la Résurrection de Jésus* (Paris: Gabalda, 1979), pp. 69–81.

23. Betz, "The Origin and Nature of Christian Faith," 41.

24. Ibid., 36.

25. Commenting on the emphatic use of "every" (literally "all" in the Greek text), A. Plummer notes that the word is used to contrast the partial or selective understandings of God's Word by the disciples; *A Critical and Exegetical Commentary on the Gospel According to Saint Luke* (Edinburgh: Clark, 1910), p. 555. In this same verse, the verb "interpret" (*diermē*) is best read as a continuing tense in Greek, suggesting an extended discourse (so Marshall, *Luke*, p. 897).

26. For the various exegetical positions and the Lucan theology of table fellowship, see the extended discussion of Guillaume, *Luc interprète*, pp. 129–59; for the eucharistic debate, ibid., pp. 129–33.

27. Ibid., pp. 118–22.

28. Ibid., pp. 80–81, 92.

29. R. Schreiter, "The Specification of Experience and the Language in Revelation," *Revelation and Experience: Concilium* 113, E. Schillebeeckx and B. Van Iersel, eds. (New York: Seabury, 1979), pp. 57–65.

30. See also Schreiter's remarks, ibid., pp. 62–63.

31. G. Bornkamm, "God's Word and Man's Word in the New Testament," *Early Christian Experience* (New York: Harper & Row, 1969), pp. 1–13; here, pp. 6–7. For similar approach from a systematic viewpoint, see C. E. Winquist, "The Sacrament of the Word of God," *Encounter* 33(1972):217–29; especially p. 229.

32. Augustine, *Confessions*, VIII, xii, 28–30, as cited in P. Brown, *Augustine of Hippo* (Berkeley: University of California, 1969), pp. 108–09.

33. For the background of this text, see B. Rigaux, *Saint Paul: Les Epîtres aux Thessaloniciens* (Paris: Gabalda, 1956), pp. 374–79; also, E. Best, *A Commentary on the First and Second Epistles to the Thessalonians* (London: Adam and Black, 1972), pp. 74–78.

34. Rigaux's reading of the Greek *plērophoria* is different ("et en abondance de toute sorte"), *Thessaloniciens*, p. 375.

35. Rigaux's comments on the total communication implied in the Greek text (*metadounai*) "share with" are helpful here; see ibid., p. 422.

36. See ibid., pp. 380–81; p. 385.
37. Rigaux sees this ecclesial dimension as a new insight of Paul that complements the older Jewish idea of imitation (ibid., p. 380).
38. RCIA, par. 9.
39. Ibid., par. 106a.
40. W. Kasper, "Wort und Symbol im sakramentalen Leben," *Bild—Wort—Symbol in der Theologie*, W. Heinen, ed. (Würzburg: Echter, 1969), pp. 157–75; here, p. 165.
41. See K. Rahner, "Vom Hören and Sehen: Eine theologische Überlegung," *Bild—Wort—Symbol in der Theologie* (supra n. 40), pp. 139–56; here, p. 147.
42. See I. Ramsey, *Religious Language* (London: SCM, 1957), especially pp. 36–38.
43. Pope Paul VI, *On Evangelization in the Modern World*, par. 13.
44. See E. Käsemann, *Commentary on Romans* (Grand Rapids: W. B. Eerdmans, 1980), pp. 293–98.
45. J. Fitzmyer, *The Gospel According to Luke I–IX* (Garden City: Doubleday, 1981), p. 702.
46. R. Schreiter, "The Specification of Experience and the Language in Revelation," pp. 57–65.
47. E. Käsemann, *Perspectives on Paul* (Philadelphia: Fortress, 1971), pp. 133–36.
48. Augustine, Tract. in Joan. 80,3, *Corpus Christianorum*, Series Latina, Vol. 36 (Turnholt: Brepols, 1954), p. 529.
49. See B. R. Brinkman, "On Sacramental Man: I. Language Patterning," *The Heythrop Journal* 13(1972):371–401; here, 387–94.
50. See C. K. Barrett, *A Commentary on the Second Epistle to the Corinthians* (New York: Harper & Row, 1975), pp. 76–80.
51. See J. Track, "Erfahrung Gottes," *Kerygma und Dogma* 22(1976):1–21; here, 12–13.
52. B. Lonergan, *Method in Theology* (New York: Herder & Herder, 1972), p. 117; also, see F. Crowe, *Theology of the Christian Word: A Study in History* (New York: Paulist, 1978), pp. 124–43.
53. Augustine, *De Trinitate*, 15, 16, 25, *Nicene and Post-Nicene Fathers*, Vol. 3 (New York: Scribner's, 1917), p. 214.

Chapter 3

HONORABLE INTENTIONS?

Are our intentions honorable? This challenge should leave both the candidates and the initiated in the Christian community unsettled. The question of our intentions goes to the very root of our lives since it scrutinizes our decisions, goals, and vision for the future. The popular saying, "The road to hell is paved with good intentions," is not accurate unless "intention" is being understood as a well-meant but consistent lack of decision. For our intentions, as the Latin origin of the word indicates, stretch us into a new position in our lives. If those intentions are indeed good, then the focus of our lives will be on the Kingdom of God. The way to the Kingdom of God is paved only with good intentions. Cyril of Jerusalem, a fourth-century bishop, has much the same message for his catechumens: God wants nothing else from us than a good intention or purpose.[1] He understands "intention" not as idle moral wishing, but as a decisive living out of the gospel way.

The Word of God, as we saw in chapter 2, challenges our intentions and calls us to reconsider our current values. The RCIA, at the crucial moment of the election of catechumens into the Church, alludes to this very connection between the Word of God and the candidates' intentions. The celebrant says to the community: "For a long time they (the catechumens) have heard the word of Christ and have attempted to shape their conduct accordingly" (RCIA, par. 145). Then the celebrant says to the catechumens: "Now that you have been hearing the voice of Christ for some time, it is for you to express your intention clearly before the whole

Church. Do you wish to receive Christ's sacraments of baptism, confirmation, and the eucharist?'' (RCIA, no. 146).

In other words, the celebrant, in the name of the Church, does not ask these candidates whether they want to be able to ''do rituals'' but rather, whether they intend what Christ intends in these sacraments. Dishonorable intentions begin with the desire for sacramental rituals that give us deceptive security and a superficial sense of continuity, but no challenge to live more honestly gospel commitments in our lives. As a rule, none of us sets out to intend dishonorably, but our unreflected decisions and values can easily deceive us into thinking that we do indeed intend as Christ intends.

The purpose of this chapter is to provide an opportunity for readers to reexamine their intentions.[2] Whether they are convinced or disenchanted Christians, catechumens or simply inquirers, everyone can learn something important about themselves and their communities, if they are willing to struggle with the question of honest intentions. The local parish or the diocesan communities must also learn how to revalue their goals and vision in the light of the Gospel. Like the extensive roots of an old tree, the story of our intentions reach out to unexpected places. Questions unasked for a long time are once again posed.

This chapter attempts to discuss honest intentionality by suggesting three related questions. First, using the scriptural metaphor of conversion, do we still ''walk'' as Christians? Second, how much do our reexamined experiences tell us about the way we intend to walk as a Christian? Finally, in what ways is the more radical sin of our lives the result of dishonest or unrealistic intentions? These questions need to be answered. Otherwise, the final irony would be the worst—the discovery that we ritualized as Christians, but never intended to be one.

The Christian Walk

Each person walks in a distinct way. A person's manner of walking may or may not resemble that of other members of the family. Most people are not even conscious of the way they walk, and yet it usually embodies a great deal more than they would care to have others know about them. The picture becomes even more complicated when we are walking with or toward someone. Unarticulated social rituals permit us to cue other walkers about who must give way. Since the body itself is a microcosm of our world, it is not surprising that the body in motion is symbolic of so much.[3]

In fact, words like "the way" and "walk" are privileged metaphors in Scripture for the choices and decisions of our lives. J. Paul Sampley summarizes this biblical usage: "To 'walk' a certain way was to live in that manner. When one's situation changed, one 'walked' differently."[4] To be asked about our "walk," then, is to be questioned about our real intentions. In turn, God's injunction, "This is the way; walk in it" (Isa. 30:21, RSV) leaves little doubt about its meaning.

In the letter to the Ephesians, the writer uses the "walk" metaphor several times in urging deeper commitment to his Christian readers. (In some English translations of the letter, the sense of the metaphor is translated as "conduct" or "live" instead of the literal translation "walk.") "Consider carefully, then, how you walk" (Eph. 5:15).[5] In the context, the writer has been discussing the practical problems of Christian living. In a vivid comparison, pagan and Christian conduct are juxtaposed so that this demand can be more forcefully made: "Accordingly, I say this and warn you in the Lord that you no longer walk as the Gentiles walk in the emptiness of their mind . . ." (Eph. 4:17).

The comparison in the letter to the Ephesians is between those who have a purposeful direction in their lives and those who do not. Some Christians had once been Gentiles both in name and lifestyle. At some point, these converts made important changes in their lives because of the message of the Cross. Their radical change of "walking" involved their priorities, their dreams, and their decisions about their future. With this change of direction also came, often enough, different people to walk with—the rich mingled with the poor, masters and mistresses with slaves, the educated with the illiterate, the washed and well-dressed with the unwashed and unkempt. We twentieth-century Christians can easily forget how radical such gatherings were where the terms "brother" and "sister" were regularly used. To walk with such a motley group was a question of intention.

The letter to the Ephesians reviews decisions once made to walk as a Christian because intentions are in constant need of reassessment. Directions in our lives initially taken often become dead-end streets. As a result, we must retrace our steps, discover what went wrong, refocus our direction. Ephesians' call is to Christians who have learned, after the initial enthusiasm, how hard the journey can be: "I exhort you, then, as a prisoner for the Lord, to walk worthily in the calling to which you have been called" (Eph. 4:1).

After more than two thousand years of use, the metaphor of "walking" has lost none of its force. The aimless direction of some Christians and candidates is in sharp contrast to the purposeful walk of others. Once again, the primary role of the Christian community is to proclaim credibly the Christian way that can become blurred in a particular social and cultural context. To "walk" as a Christian teenager in the late twentieth century, for example, represents something radically different in Poland, in Zaire, and in North America.

Another way of describing this problem is to ask whether the sacraments of initiation are being confused with other rites of passage in our American society.[6] A driver's license and the right to order a drink are identified as rites of passage by some American teenagers. A full-time job and buying one's first car are seen as similar transitional rites by some of America's young adults. The frequently unexamined assumptions and expectations of both the young and their elders are built into such rites.

As Victor Turner and other anthropologists have shown, if rites of passage are celebrated in a well-structured group, then not only the young candidates but the whole community benefits in terms of greater social cohesion, rethinking of roles, and a reexamined sense of direction.[7] The positive impact of rites of passage for a teenager, for example, in some increasingly Westernized areas of Asia or Africa still renew the family or larger group initiating the candidates.

Religious rites of passage in the United States, however, present a more complicated picture. Familiar transitional rituals such as infant baptism, first communion, confirmation, and marriage tend to blend in with other public rituals of American life (for example, graduations and anniversaries). Too often religious rites of passage are celebrated in loosely structured families or institutional parishes.[8] The theological and pastoral result is that the prophetic role of the sacramental rites of passage, such as the sacraments of initiation, is either considerably reduced in meaning or totally secularized. The Christian "walk" becomes a casual and noncommitted stroll.

In the introductory rite of becoming a catechumen, the celebrant says to the candidates: "You have *followed* his light. Now *the way of the Gospel* opens before you. . . . This is *the way of faith* on which Christ will lovingly guide you to eternal life. Are you ready *to enter on this path* under the leadership of Christ?" (RCIA, no. 76). The scriptural metaphor of the "walk" is continually improvised upon in this catechumenal address in order to urge the candidates and the baptized to deepen their commitment. In contemporary language, the catechumens are asked to "buy into" God's vision of life and its purpose as embodied in Christ, and thus, to become Christians. Not surprisingly, even in these initial rituals, candidates are challenged to certain commitments as were earlier candidates in the community of Hippolytus in third-century Rome.

Hippolytus instructs the ministry of the community: "There should be an inquiry about the work and professions of those who have been presented for instruction: if anyone is a brothel-keeper, he will stop or be sent away. If anyone is a sculptor or painter, they are to be instructed not to make idols; they are to stop or be sent away. . . . The same for the chariot-driver who races or those who take part in the public games. . . . The soldier who is in charge shall not kill anyone. If he receives the order, he shall not execute it and he shall not take the military oath."[9] Hippolytus' community was trying to deal in a practical fashion with the problem that we discussed above—assuring the Christian meaning of commitment in the catechumenal rites of passage.

By definition, God's mystery, that is, his active and saving presence, is not prisoner to our theories and observations. Even in the most disappointing pastoral situation, we cannot dismiss his quiet work in the lives of people and the community as a whole. God enables us to "walk" as children of the light. The complementary side of this gift, however, is our response, which takes the shape of our intention. Two people, for example, can send a Mother's Day card: one out of guilt, the other out of a freely given love. The action of sending the card is externally the same. The intention in each case is quite different.

Cyril of Jerusalem offers a similar example to his catechumens, that of Simon Magus (Acts 8:9–24). Like the Samaritans, Simon is baptized, "but not enlightened." In Cyril's concise analysis, "His body went down and came up; but his soul was not buried with Christ, nor with him raised."[10] We touch the core of the challenge of initiating. Will we, like Simon, share only in the rituals of Christ, or will we have the same mind or intention as Christ (Phil. 2:5)?

The Intention to Walk

William James, in his classic *The Varieties of Religious Experience*, takes the scene of Augustine's conversion in his Confessions which we discussed in the last chapter. Augustine hears the words, "Take up and read" that day in the garden. James is illustrating his famous notion of the divided self by Augustine's analysis of his situation: "the evil to which I was so accustomed held me more than the better life I had not tried."[11] In a subsequent chapter on conversion, James returns to this example in Augustine's life once more in order to analyze the ways in which we may remain a divided self: "A less complete way is the simultaneous coexistence of two or more different groups of aims, of which one practically holds the right of way and instigates activity, whilst the others are only pious wishes, and never practically come to anything."[12]

In Augustine's life as in our own, the aims that hold the "right of way," to use James' phrase, can impede us from walking the right way. In trying to isolate and examine such aims, James uses an illuminating metaphor: "the hot place in man's consciousness, the group of ideas to which he devotes himself, and from which he works . . . *the habitual center of his personal energy*."[13]

The Word of God uncovers this precise but often unexamined area of ourselves—our intentions. Intentionality includes the "why" of our activity. In other words, behind the attention and actions of our lives, there is always a frame or focus that actively directs the way we take in our lives.[14] James' description of this focal area of ourselves as "the hot place" is indeed apt. Why we choose to love or hate, to be selfless or selfish, to be responsible or irresponsible is always related to this intentionality. We respond to and structure our world by the way we intend.[15] God's presence-filled Word challenges this center of meaning that shapes the knowing and willing of our lives.

If we are to be identified as Christian by more than the rituals we use, then we must be willing to discover the real purpose and operational aims of our lives. Why are we still Christian or wish to become one? Why do we choose to be sober, honest, or chaste? Why do we stay married or faithful to our religious vows? Why does the Christian community want to receive candidates into initiation? Such questions do not admit of simple answers. But these and similar questions must be dealt with, however, if we wish to be on the way to the Kingdom.

The "Yes" and "No" of Living

Some parents are convinced that the first word a small child learns to say is not "Mommie" or "Daddy" but "No." "Yes" and "No" articulate what we choose.[16] These one-syllable words are powerful because they represent the tension in every choice, and are often the preface to a set of actions that reveal our real selves.[17] In a penetrating description of Jesus, Paul says: "Jesus Christ . . . was not alternately 'Yes' and 'No'; he was never anything but 'Yes'" (2 Cor. 1:19). The decisive and focused purpose of Jesus' life and death is summarized in that brief word "Yes" in the earliest strata of traditions about the historical Jesus; it captures his attitude of filial obedience to his Father throughout a lifetime.

Our words and rituals, however, can be deceptive, if not deceitful. The parable of Jesus about the two sons illustrates this very point. The elder son, in reply to his father's request that he work in the vineyard, says "'I am on my way, sir'; but he never went" (Matt. 21:29). This man either has not sorted out his priorities (and is therefore deceiving himself), or knows what he wants (and chooses to deceive others). Most of us do not choose to be deceitful; we are simply selectively blind to our real aims and interests. In counseling and therapy, people initially cannot "see" their true motivation in certain key incidents in their lives. The way in which they recount a particular story reflects this blindness to their real intentions.[18]

Our "Yes" and "No" ultimately spell out the meanings that we consider central to our lives. Even dictionaries define "intention" in terms of meaning as well as purpose. *Meaning, in the last analysis, is what keeps us going and growing in our lives.*[19] In focused and thoughtful living, there is always an intimate link between our meanings and our intentions. When parents, for example, say that their children *mean* everything to them, they are presumably also indicating some of the aims and motives of their own lives. Intention, then, should represent our implementation of the meanings that give scope and purpose to our very existence. To put it differently, we cannot live meaningfully without having commitment.[20] When Paul says that Jesus "was never anything but 'Yes'" (2 Cor. 1:19), the apostle is underlining the central meaning of Christ's life, and offering that meaning as a model for the Christian.

Catechumenal Conversion and the Search for Meaning

In a profound sense, the catechumenate is a process in which Christ's meaning begins to challenge our intentions. I have argued in the previous chapter that the Word of God is his dynamic presence questioning our meanings. When we accept to sit "at the table of God's Word" (to cite again the beautiful phrase of the RCIA), we indicate a willingness to enter a process of conversion. At the heart of this process is a renewed attention to what motivates our lives and to what extent this agrees with God's priorities as embodied in Jesus Christ. If our actions are to be truly Christian, then our meanings and intentions must correspond to those of Christ.

An important theological and pastoral question is how to implement the catechumenal process in such a way that the complex meanings of our lives are laid bare and that both the baptized and the candidates may be strengthened to choose Christ's meaning and act upon it. As already indicated more than once, this is not accomplished by theoretical formulations, but by the living Word that presents both the praxis and theory of God among us.

R. Doran maintains that "psychic conversion," as an extension of B. Lonergan's theological method, should help in narrating our story of commitment to promote the human good "by authentic performance at all levels of intentional consciousness."[21] This narration of our meanings and intentions begins with the complex network of experience on the affective, intellectual, and embodied levels of our personality. Faced with this complexity, we must learn to decipher the symbols that capture our experience and, as a result, to make certain changes in the way we think and act.

If I return to a key narrative, for example, in which I describe my failure to earn a much sought-after writing certificate in my first week of grammar school, I must retrieve more than the facts of the incident.[22] I must capture the other dimensions of the same experience: the feelings of shame, confusion, and anxiety, intensified by the general uncertainty of this new situation and life-stage, my early school experience. The meanings I gave to this highly coded incident in my life in the past, as well as my current evaluation of it, are vital to the way in which I focus my human energy to be as fully Christian as I can be. Even such simple narratives of my life include the complex outline of my intentions and meanings. If I wish to intend what Christ intends, I cannot afford to be ignorant of the stories of my past intentions and meanings.

The way in which this process of narrative response to the Word of God is implemented in a particular catechumenate obviously needs to be accommodated to the specific culture and people involved. The catechumenal team (whom we shall discuss in more detail in the next chapter) must be capable of modeling the process for candidates. Above all, the larger community of the baptized needs to participate in this same experience of having their own intentions and meanings clarified by the Word of God. The Sunday liturgy of the Word, for example, is a rich pastoral opportunity for initiating Christians into a narrative response to God's Word.

A Curious Story

There is more than one story in the Gospels that follows the pattern of 1) the discovery of who Jesus is; 2) personal reevaluation; 3) a response of praise and confession; 4) some subsequent commitment. Behind such a pattern, there are the underlying questions that touch the lives of the people in the story. The final thrust of these stories always seems to be a clarification of intentions of these people. Such gospel stories illustrate the process of assisting catechumens and the baptized to understand more clearly their intentions. Moreover, the pattern behind such gospel stories reflects the process of insight, judgment, and decision discussed above. We turn to one such story as a model for this process.

The story of the miraculous catch of fishes has two different settings in the Gospels. In John's gospel, this story is part of the postresurrection accounts (John 21:1–14). In Luke's gospel, however, the scene occurs at the beginning of Jesus' public ministry (Luke 5:1–11).[23] Luke evocatively pictures Jesus preaching to the crowds from a boat belonging to a man named Simon. When Jesus has finished his discourse, he gives Simon a strange summons: put out into deeper water and lower the nets for a catch. The experienced Simon objects that they had been doing this all night with no success, but he obliges Jesus. Simon and his crew are rewarded with such a great catch of fish that their boats nearly sink.

The climax of the story, which Luke has skillfully prepared, is yet to come. Simon falls at the knees of Jesus and says: "Leave me, Lord. I am a sinful man." Jesus' response goes beyond Simon's words: "Do not be afraid. From now on you will be catching men" (Luke 5:8, 10). The final line of Luke's account is a verification of Jesus' words: Simon along with James and John, leaves everything and follows his new master.

R. Pesch, in his extensive study of this story, points out that Simon's new self-awareness ("I am a sinner") is the consequence of a discovery: Jesus is Lord. Luke, in effect, gives us an epiphany or revelation-scene in which Jesus is shown to be more than a gifted itinerant preacher. The technical term "Lord" (Greek: *Kurios*) is employed as an act of confession and proclamation: the Savior is here.[24] The response of Jesus deals with Simon's self-acknowledgment as a sinner in an unexpected way—the invitation to discipleship. The surprising element of Luke's story, then, is not the miraculous catch of fish, but the unexpected call to discipleship of such flawed people as Simon and his response of commitment.[25]

One suspects that long before the oral traditions of the early Church about Jesus were finally written down, the stories about Simon Peter and Jesus exercised a great influence among converts to Christianity. In both Luke's and John's differing accounts of this particular event, for example, Peter emerges as a powerful paradigm of conversion and commitment. There is an intimate connection between the awareness and acknowledgment of who Jesus is and the self-awareness of Peter. This process of self-awareness is tied to the question of intention that we have been discussing throughout this chapter. Peter's confession of Jesus as Lord would have little meaning if that title were not verified in the reassessed direction of the fisherman's own life. Peter did, in fact, leave the security of what he knew and possessed, and throw in his lot with Jesus.

Catechumenal learning entails a new examination of our intentions. The traditional guideline for a valid sacrament, "to intend as the Church intends," is a development, from a theological point of view, of the Pauline sentiment, to intend as Christ intends. It is interesting to note that in the choice of readings for the Lenten period with its immediate concerns about the preparation of the catechumens for the initiation rites of Easter, the Christian community was making a final effort to assist candidates and the baptized alike to reexamine their lives.[26] In our current lectionary, the scriptural readings for the Sundays of Lent, in particular, still reflect this concern. Even if the specific gospel reading does not follow the pattern of the four steps mentioned above, these steps may still serve as useful way of hearing and responding to God's Word in an intentional way.

The Word of God, as mentioned in chapter 2, is the presence of God. In other words, when the Scriptures are proclaimed, there is a true epiphany or revelation of who Jesus is. We are not deprived of the experience of Jesus as Lord that brought Peter to his knees. Moreover, to be in the presence of the Lord is to perceive our own life-situation in a new context. It is not important that we know the specific details that caused Peter to see himself as a sinner. The important insights of our lives do not always have footnotes attached to them. A new look at the directions and values of our lives is often the result of a hitherto unseen profile of certain decisions (for example, the sudden awareness that our family's or spouse's life has always had to fit into our own career plans and ambitions).

R. Schreiter has pointed out that a specification of experience is a movement from the known to the unknown.[27] This description not only applies to the way in which Jesus is perceived in the New Testament, but also to the intuitive leaps that open up our perspective. This was the experience of a young Francis of Assisi who heard the familiar gospel command to sell all and give to the poor as a new and vital direction for his own life. When the contexts of our lives frame the texts of God's Word, epiphany is never far off. That which was familiar becomes new. As in all creative learning, we begin to ask disclosing questions rather than resting content with our pat answers.

As we move away from the secure interpretations we have given our reasons and motives, decisions and goals, our need for Christ, like Peter's, reasserts itself in a new key. From such awareness new praise of God in Christ can take shape. Peter's confession of Jesus as Lord is a model that Luke offers his community. Peter, in Luke's account, is not reciting a doctrinal statement about Jesus as Lord. Rather, his words of recognition of Jesus are a prayer that do indicate saving doctrine (the law of worship is the law of belief).

Catechumenal Learning

The miraculous catch of fishes is, then, an important clue to the connection between the liturgical and doctrinal formation or re-education of the Christian. The Church teaches what she has experienced of God's salvation in our midst. This emphasis on the saving praxis of God on our behalf does not devalue theological theory. Rather, it is another way of saying that the Christian church experienced and celebrated God as Trinity, for example, before she attempted to articulate a doctrinal statement in response to heresy about the inner life of God. The Church could witness to the saving work of a Risen Lord in her midst long before there were christologies attempting to clarify the nature and work of Christ.

The Word of God is a process that leads us to discovery, awareness, personal reevaluation, and praise. Within this process there is always an important place for learning the rich insight that the Church's experience of God has forged. Doctrine becomes alive and relevant in the Christian's and catechumen's life when it flows from the experience of God and leads back to that experience. A well-known legend about two of the Church's great doctors and saints of the thirteenth century might illustrate this point. Bonaventure and Thomas Aquinas are depicted as asking one another where they had acquired their great theological knowledge. The answer is a silent gesture toward the crucifix on the wall.

Authentic Christian experience and knowledge always result in renewed discipleship. This discipleship, in turn, should prompt us to return to theology with new respect and love. Again, Francis of Assisi gives us an example when he tells his brothers to respect theologians because they teach people the Word of God.

Throughout this chapter I have been arguing for a more realistic view of conversion, in response to God's Word as a radical reevaluation of the major choices and directions of our lives, that is, intentionality. A corollary to this line of thought is that true Christian learning and doctrine result from and are productive of the Christian's experience of God. I should like to offer one concluding example of this catechumenal approach, applied to those already baptized.

Recently, as a visiting professor at a large university, I had the opportunity to teach undergraduates a course in the theology of the eucharist after twelve years of teaching the same course to graduate students majoring in theology. The undergraduates were obviously a very different audience than the graduate students for a number of reasons. For the college students, there was an academic requirement of fulfilling certain theological course credits and of getting a good grade in a highly competitive school. In other words, the major concern of many of these students was academic success, not necessarily a question of conversion and intentionality. Furthermore, some of their previous experiences of the eucharist on Sunday prejudiced their attitude on the value of the course.

As a teacher, I could opt for a spirited theological presentation of the eucharist that would, one hopes, be interesting and intelligent. Another option was to start with a belief that God had already touched the lives of these students many times. The question of

Christ's presence and self-gift in the eucharist could not be separated from the question of their own presence and the intentionality that shaped it.

I opted for the latter approach and gradually reviewed with them their experience of God at the same time that we examined the theology of eucharistic presence. There is always an initial resistance, I find, to this approach because it demands much more than good note-taking and perceptive analysis. We do not always welcome epiphany, self-awareness, praise of God, and the ensuing renewed commitment in our lives because the process can be costly. But I was not disappointed. Gradually the theoretical teaching on the eucharist began to have relevance for many students because it had been preceded and accompanied by connections with their own retrieved experience of God and others. I saw a process taking place in at least some students' lives that resembled the Lucan sequence of discipleship which I have been describing.

Liturgical Intentionality

The Word of God teaches us honest liturgy because it prepares us to symbolize "knowingly, actively, and fruitfully" (*Constitution on the Sacred Liturgy*, I, par. 11). As catechumens learn to respond to God's Word out of their revealed need, they begin to use the words and gestures of prayer. If we surveyed the liturgical formation of catechumens in the third or fourth century, the thirteenth century, and in our post–Vatican II era, we might expect to find certain perduring rituals and some fascinating differences. The third-century catechumen, for example, might learn to pray with arms extended; the thirteenth-century convert might find genuflection and kneeling an important ritual, while standing for the post–Vatican II catechumen is a common posture of prayer. But liturgical formation deals with the attitudes, experience, and decisions with which we must cry out to God. This type of formation is a common heritage for the Christians of every age.

Intentionality, as we have been describing it, bridges the personal experience of the catechumen or baptized and the shared prayer and worship of the larger Christian community. For both, liturgical celebration and private prayer of the believer are under the scrutiny of one criterion: do we intend as Christ intends? Expressed differently, have our decisions and vision in life been shaped by those of Christ? To answer such a question, both the Christian community and the individual bring to liturgy what they are and what they do. Liturgy, as a symbolic action, honestly participated in, clarifies the unexamined and the known motives and reasons behind our actions and decisions. The Bishops' statement on *Music in Catholic Worship* is one of the clearest summaries of this process in liturgical intentionality: "We are celebrating when we involve ourselves meaningfully in the thoughts, words, songs, and gestures of the worshipping community . . . *when we mean the words and want to do what is done. . . . To celebrate liturgy means to do the action or perform the sign in such a way that the full meaning and impact shine forth in clear and compelling fashion.*"[28]

"To mean what we do" brings us to the heart of the Christian morality. Should there be anything specifically different about the moral attitudes and actions of a catechumen or baptized person? Is Christian accountability simply a baptized version of the ten commandments or the natural law? Is Christian morality, in effect, only a stricter set of rules than an ancient Stoic moralist or a contemporary ethical agnostic might have?

Children of Light

Before Paul tackles some of the thorny moral questions within the Corinthian community, he flatly states: "The Kingdom of God does not consist in talk but in power" (1 Cor. 4:20).[29] As already indicated, this power is a transforming and directive force in the life of the Christian community. When Paul approaches the practical moral problems at Corinth of incest, and other sexual issues, of lawsuits, and of scandal, he has a larger specifically Christian frame of reference within which to discuss these matters.

It would be outside the scope and competence of this book to discuss the complicated development and individual issues of Christian morality. On the other hand, we cannot evade a central question of Christian initiation: Do Christians "walk" differently from other good but unbelieving people? Paul, after all, firmly states that the basic moral law of God should be visible even to a pagan (Rom. 1:18–

19). The result of ignoring this law is a people "without consci-ence, without loyalty, without pity" (Rom. 1:31).[30]

If the reader has carefully followed the discussions on the Cross of Christ and the Word of God, then their implications for Christian thought and action should be evident. Although the early Christian church did not hesitate to adapt and transform existing moral norms,[31] the specific difference of an authentic Christian morality is the Kingdom of God, as Paul noted. In the parables of Jesus and in the preaching of the early Church, God's Kingdom is proclaimed as the meaning of our existence and the test of our honesty.

One of the aims of the extended period of catechumenal formation envisaged by the RCIA, as we already noted, is "a progressive change of outlook and morals . . . together with its social conse-quences" (RCIA, par. 19, no. 2). The Word of God and the Word from the Cross inevitably reveal the need for change. Origen graph-ically describes this process to his catechumens of the third century as a journey in which they have come through the Red Sea in order to listen to the law of God and gaze, like Moses, on the glory of God daily.[32] But even this journey would lose its ultimate meaning without the reminder of the Our Father—"Thy Kingdom come"—and our responsibility for sharing in its actualization.

The Kingdom of God is marked by a unity that we have yet to experience. The reign of sin, on the other hand, is visible in the disunity of our world and our lives. No one may remain a passive observer of this cosmic struggle between God's promise and sin's solutions. Whether we are discussing the morality of nuclear war, environmental issues, Third World famine, abortion, sexuality, or business praxis, the underlying issue is whether we are "slaves" of sin or of God, as Paul puts it (Rom. 6:20, 22). In real life, Christian morality is always enfleshed in a person or community deciding to witness to God's kingdom of peace and unity in their own historical era.

Paul frames the moral actions of the Christian community and its members in one word—freedom (*eleutheria*). As we saw in chapter 1, the law can paradoxically reinforce the sinful situations of human existence. But authentic freedom for Paul is the door to God's reign. To the baptized Romans Paul says: "The law of the spirit, the spirit of life in Christ Jesus, has freed you from the law of sin and death'' (Rom. 8:2). This radically new possibility allows Christians to be free, like Christ, to give themselves unselfishly for others.[33] Origen's image of the journey of the Jewish people to freedom, then, is an appropriate one for describing the initiation experience.

Paul thanks God that the Roman Christians who are living the "rule of teaching which was imparted to you" (Rom. 6:17) are now free. In fact, these Christians have become "weapons for justice" (Rom. 6:13). The underlying metaphor is the battle that is waged between God and evil. In their decision to live the gospel teaching, Christians have died to what bound them (Rom. 7:6) and are at liberty to announce the Gospel to others.[34]

In other words, the moral teaching of Christ, as expressed in Paul and elsewhere in the New Testament, is always addressed to the disciple of Christ. This statement is far from being obvious if the moral praxis of many Christians is scrutinized. There can be a costly difference between the Kingdom perspective of a disciple of Christ and the ethical perspective of nominal Christians or good-living agnostics. This contention is based on the very nature of Christ's own mission and person: he did not call two groups to follow him—disciples and nominal Christians. To "walk" as a Christian, then, is to learn to live the vision of the Master that proclaims and prepares God's Kingdom. A morality apart from this vision is not yet Christian.

Who Are the Blessed?

In both the gospels of Matthew (especially chapters 5–7) and of Luke (especially chapter 6), we have examples of the disciples learning to be like the Master. Commenting on Matthew's presentation of Christ's moral teaching, John P. Meier correctly points out that the constant frame of reference for this teaching is the nature of Christ (christology) and of the Church (ecclesiology).[35] When we turn to the Sermon on the Mount and its recital of the Beatitudes, for example, we see graphically etched out the moral vision of a disciple of Christ.

Matthew gives his community the picture of Jesus seated on the mountainside, teaching the art of discipleship. The promise made to authentic disciples is summed up in a refrain that resonates throughout the Beatitudes—"The reign of God is theirs" (Matt. 5:3–12). In language reminiscent of the Old Testament, Jesus begins an astonishing enumeration of who are the truly "blessed": the poor in spirit, the sorrowing and lowly, those who cannot have enough of God, the merciful, the persecuted, and the peacemakers.[36] One hears the visionary lines of Isaiah (61:1–3) about the servant anointed to proclaim the good news and liberty, to heal the brokenhearted, and to comfort mourners, transposed into a major and triumphant tonality. Above all, Jesus' words are striking because they are personified in himself. "The Beatitudes mirror Jesus himself, the truly happy man, the embodiment of the joy the Kingdom brings."[37]

In effect, Jesus presents a positive starting point for morality: the power of God's unearned love enables ordinary people to deal with the complexity of an imperfect and sinful historical situation with God's purpose and meaning. In succeeding lines of the Sermon on the Mount, Jesus describes disciples as "salt of the earth" and "light of the world." The very moral goodness of the Christian must serve to announce credibly God's Kingdom—"so that they may see goodness in your acts and give praise to your heavenly Father" (Matt. 5:16). Matthew then continues in chapters 5 and 6 to outline the more specific moral issues of anger, impurity, divorce, oaths, retaliation, love of enemies, and the question of underlying motivation.[38]

In other words, Jesus gives one way of "walking" as a Christian—discipleship. That discipleship is modeled on Jesus' own vision and proclamation of his Father's Kingdom. The morality of disciples is inseparably linked to a profound freedom to be what God has created each person to be—a unique, gifted, and loving witness to his "new creation."[39] There is no moral question that touches the life of the Christian community or its individual members which does not also affect the honesty and urgency of their prayer: "Your Kingdom come" (Matt. 6:10). Without the deepening commitment of discipleship and the growing awareness of the purpose of our gifts, Christian morality will remain a set of rules and not God's vision of what it means to be "blessed."

Catechumenal Accountability

There are many "moral majorities" among us these days. Each group represents a moral stance that it characterizes as "Christian." Whether the case in point is abortion, pornography, military defense, or environmental issues, the basic argument revolves around assumptions of what it means to be Christian. Likewise, in our preaching and teaching, we must deal with the specific moral problems of premarital sex of young people, of divorce, of social injustice questions, and so forth. Again, we presume that our definition of being "Christian" is correct. But does the Kingdom of God figure in our assumptions about Christian morality?

The challenge of initiation invites us, catechumens and baptized alike, to listen humbly to God's Word once again. God help us if we teach others to do the right thing for the wrong reason. Initiation teaches us all to "walk" as disciples toward the Kingdom of God. Conversion, then, is not simply an external change of actions, but rather a radical revision of attitude. In Matthew's gospel, for example, there is a major concern about a subtle species of "lawlessness" that refuses to accept God's vision. Matthew addresses this problem as one of the Pharisee and of the superficial Christian.[40] It is within this context that the ringing impact of Jesus' words must be understood: "Let me make it clear that tax collectors and prostitutes are entering the kingdom of God before you" (Matt. 21:31).[41]

To answer our opening question, "Are your intentions honorable?" we must ask whether the radical vision of Jesus about his Father's Kingdom is the operative principle in our communal and personal praxis, not just our moral theory. We must also ask if our formation as Christians is consistently shaped within this overarching principle, "Your Kingdom come."

Some Conclusions

To inculcate this larger moral vision in our preaching, teaching, and living, we must begin with some of the issues that we broached in chapter 1. First, blessed is the Christian community or individual who shares with Christ "the originating value" of the Cross. If we, like Paul, prize the meaning and power of the Cross, we will live in such a way as to prepare for the Kingdom of God. We will value what Jesus values and thus, be "like-minded." When this principle is applied to specific issues, such as sexuality or social justice, there will be a constant need for greater generosity and more radical love. On the other hand, when there exists a tolerated dichotomy within the local church between a demanding teaching in sexual matters and an equivocal position in matters of social justice and nuclear disarmament, then what is the originating value, in praxis, within that community?

Second, if the Christian community is to be "martyr," that is, witness, then it must relearn its prophetic tasks in this world. A Christian morality, forged by Jesus' vision of the Kingdom, is not a search for the lowest common moral denominator. While neither rigid nor harsh, Jesus' descriptions of the truly "blessed" person are hardly to be confused with the polite, conventional, or even heroic ethical positions of someone who does not believe that there is a Kingdom of God. Christian morality has the distinct mission of symbolizing what the new Jerusalem will be like. The book of Revelation speaks of the Kingdom as if it had the Beatitudes in view: "There shall be no more death or mourning, crying out or pain" (Rev. 21:4).

In pastoral terms, this may spell out different priorities within the Christian community. Do adult Christians, for example, witness gospel values to younger Christians in selective moral areas (for example, insistence on a responsible sexual morality, but an indifference to social injustice in their own community)? Does the catechumenal formation and Sunday preaching to the baptized only address "safe" issues that will not disturb the complacency of an affluent or a socially biased community?

Third, an authentic Christian morality focuses on the Christian sense of time. Unchristian ways of thinking and acting are usually supported by a selfish view of time. The Kingdom of God redefines why we have been given the gift of time. God's future makes us reexamine our present. In effect, Jesus' parables about the Kingdom of God change our perception, in surprising ways, of what use we should make of the time we have left and of how gratuitous the gift of each day is. In our postindustrial society with its mechanized sense of time, an eschatological view will demand more generosity and responsibility both from the young person who may feel that he or she has "all the time in the world" and from the elderly for whom time can be a fleeting and frightening measure of their own limits.

●

NOTES

1. *The Protochesis*, par. 8. The Greek text can be found in edited version by Cross, *The Christian Sacraments*, supra chap. 2, n. 4, p. 5.
2. This chapter attempts to develop a line of thought that I began in other writings; see *Real Presence*, pp. 90–91; "Formative Experience and Intentional Liturgy," *Studies in Formative Spirituality* 3(1982):351–61; *A Roman Catholic Theology of Pastoral Care*, pp. 88–90.
3. M. Douglas, *Natural Symbols: Explorations in Cosmology* (New York: Pantheon, 1970).
4. J. P. Sampley, "The Letter to the Ephesians," *Ephesians, Colossians, 2 Thessolonians, The Pastoral Epistles*, G. Krodel, ed. (Philadelphia: Fortress, 1978), p. 14.
5. This and other Ephesian passages are a more literal translation of the Greek text.
6. See D. Borobio, "The 'Four Sacraments' of Popular Religiosity: A Critique," *Liturgy and Human Passage: Concilium 112*, D. Power and L. Maldonado, eds. (New York: Seabury, 1979), pp. 85–97.
7. V. Turner, *The Ritual Process* (Chicago: Aldine, 1969); idem, "Passages, Margins and Poverty: Religious Symbols of Communitas," *Worship* 46(1972):390–412; 482–94; here, 402–03; A. Pasquier, "Initiation and Society," *Structures of Initiation in Crisis: Concilium 122*, L. Maldonado and D. Powers, eds. (New York: Seabury, 1979), pp. 3–13.
8. See Douglas, *Natural Symbols*, pp. 14–36, though I do not agree with some of the theological corollaries that the author seems to draw from this material.
9. *Apostolic Tradition*, par. 16; in the critical edition of B. Botte, *La Tradition Apostolique de Saint Hippolyte: Essai de reconstitution* (Münster: Aschendorff, 1963), pp. 34–37. The article of P. de Puniet is still both classic and useful; see "Catéchuménat," *Dictionnaire d'Archéologie chrétienne et de Liturgie*, II, 2579–2621.
10. See Cyril of Jerusalem, *The Protocatechesis*, par. 2 in *The Christian Sacraments*, pp. 40–41. The "enlightened" was also a term for the catechumen in the final stages of preparation (ibid., xxi–xxii). From an exegetical point of view, Cyril's analysis is quite accurate; see, for example, Dunn, *Baptism in the Holy Spirit*, pp. 55–68.
11. W. James (London: Longmans, Green, 1903), pp. 171–72.
12. Ibid., p. 194.
13. Ibid., p. 196 (James's emphasis).
14. See G. Langford, *Human Action* (Garden City, N.Y.: Doubleday, 1971), pp. 70–71.
15. R. May, *Love and Will* (New York: Norton, 1969), p. 233.
16. See S. Arieti, *The Will to Be Human* (New York: Quadrangle, 1972), p. 12.

17. May, *Love and Will*, pp. 236–38.
18. Ibid., p. 231.
19. For a review of the philosophical positions on "meaning," see J. Rychlak, *Discovering Free Will and Personal Responsibility* (New York: Oxford University, 1979), pp. 50–67; for a similar treatment of intention, see R. Lawrence, *Motive and Intention* (Evanston: Northwestern University, 1972), especially pp. 83–130.
20. May, *Love and Will*, p. 230. R. Doran expresses it from the viewpoint of a theological methodology in this way: "Transcendental method offers a reflexive technique by means of which consciousness is able to bring operations as intentional to bear upon the operations as conscious"; *Psychic Conversion and Theological Foundations*, p. 16.
21. Ibid., p. 142.
22. I discussed this from Erickson's viewpoint in *Real Presence*, pp. 64–66.
23. For an exegetical and critical comparison of the two accounts, see R. Pesch, *Der reiche Fischfang (Lk 5, 1–11/Jo 21, 1–14)* (Düsseldorf: Patmos, 1969).
24. So, for example, ibid., p. 117; also, E. Ellis, *The Gospel of Luke* (Edinburgh: Nelson, 1966), p. 102; I. H. Marshall, *The Gospel of Luke*, p. 205.
25. Ellis, *Luke*, p. 103.
26. For a discussion of these connections, see A. Baumstark, *Liturgie Comparée*, revised by B. Botte (Chevetogne: Edition de Chevetogne, 1953), pp. 211–13; J. Wilkinson, *Egeria's Travels* (London: SPCK, 1971), pp. 61–66; 144–45; G. Dix, *The Shape of the Liturgy* (London: Dacre, 1945), pp. 360–61; for the baptized Christians' part in this final stage of the catechumenal process, see ibid., pp. 354–57.
27. R. Schreiter, "Specification of Experience and the Language in Revelation," pp. 60–61.
28. *Music in Catholic Worship* (Washington, D.C.: Bishops' Committee on the Liturgy, 1972), I, 3, 7, p. 1 (italics mine).
29. For the background, see W. Meeks, *The First Urban Christians: The Social World of the Apostle Paul* (New Haven: Yale, 1963), pp. 117–31.
30. See the excellent discussion of A. Nygren, *Commentary on Romans* (Philadelphia: Fortress, 1949), pp. 101–09; somewhat differently, U. Wilckens, *Der Brief an die Römer* (Zurich: Benziger, 1978), pp. 103–05.
31. For example, the laws of households as seen in Col. 3:18, 4:1; Eph. 5:22, 6:9; 1 Pet. 2:18, 3:7. For discussion and bibliography, see K. Thraede, "Zum historischen Hintergrund der 'Haustafeln' des NT," *Pietas: Festschrift für Bernhard Kötting*, E. Dassmann and K. S. Frank, eds. (Münster: Aschendorff, 1980), pp. 359–68; for a point of comparison with pagan "pietas," see H. Dörrie, "Überlegungen zum Wesen antiker Frömmigkeit," *Pietas*, pp. 3–13.
32. As cited in H. J. Auf der Maur and J. Waldram, "Illuminatio Verbi Dei—Confessio Fidei—Gratia Baptismi. Wort, Glaube and Sakrament in Katechumenat und Taufliturgie bei Origenes," *Fides Sacramenti, Sacramentum Fidei*, H. J. Auf der Maur et al., eds. (Assen, Netherlands: Van Gorcum, 1981), pp. 41–95; here, p. 51, n. 46. The whole article is a valuable survey of Origen's catechumenate.
33. See H. Schlier, *eleutheria, Theological Dictionary of the New Testament*, 2:487–502; here, 499.

34. See H. Halter, *Taufe und Ethos: Paulinische Kriterien für das Proprium christlicher Moral* (Freiburg: Herder, 1977), pp. 69–71. Halter is correct in insisting that this teaching (Rom. 6:17) has a baptismal emphasis on the crucified and risen Lord that invites candidates into a concrete and precise moral commitment (ibid., pp. 80–81).

35. Meier, *The Vision of Matthew*, pp. 42–51.

36. In addition to the monumental three-volume study of J. Dupont, *Les Béatitudes* (Paris: Gabalda, 1969–73), see the application of the Beatitudes to moral theology in P. Hoffman and V. Eid, *Jesus von Nazareth und eine christliche Moral* (Freiburg: Herder, 1975).

37. Meier, *The Vision of Matthew*, p. 63.

38. Ibid., pp. 222–64.

39. Also, Hoffman and Eid, *Jesus von Nazareth*, pp. 68–72.

40. Meier, *The Vision of Matthew*, p. 161.

41. For a discussion of how the early Fathers of the Church used this and similar biblical images of conversion, see J. Frickel, "Die Zöllner, Vorbild der Demut und wahrer Gottesverehrung," *Pietas*, supra n. 31, pp. 369–80.

Chapter 4

THE STRETCHING OF
THE CATECHUMEN

In the middle of the fifth century, Pope Leo the Great sums up in one of his letters why Easter is a symbol for all that God does among us: "The paschal feast [is that] in which the mystery of human salvation is so completely contained."[1] Fifteen hundred years later, the introduction of the RCIA takes up the same theme in discussing the interconnection between the candidates and the initiated in a Christian community: "Together with the catechumens, the faithful reflect upon the value of the paschal mystery, renew their own conversion, and by their example lead the catechumens to obey the Holy Spirit more generously" (RCIA, par. 4).

In chapter 1, we insisted that the Church is gathered in the shadow of the Cross of Christ. The Church is the "body of Christ" as a result of Christ's self-gift on that Cross. The Christian community's values, its sense of the sacred, and its ability to witness cannot be separated from the power of the Cross. In chapter 2, the Word of God is presented as a process in which the meaning of a crucified and risen Lord questions the meanings of our lives. To hear God's Word is to "walk" toward the Kingdom of God. This metaphor of conversion as "walk," moreover, implies the willingness to "be sent," that is, to do the work of the Gospel and to praise God honestly along the way. These implications of gospel conversion inevitably led us, in chapter 3, to the question of our intentionality—the profile of our motives, goals, and decisions that constitute the core of our living. Gospel morality is a question of being of the same "mind" as Christ.

In brief, the catechumenal process uncovers some of the crucial links between the Cross, the Word of God, and the living of the Gospel. These connections are, first and foremost, a question of praxis, not theory. Both candidates and baptized are measured by the way in which they welcome these challenges of initiation and, as a result, continue to respond to the change of conversion to which God constantly call us. If there is one expression which captures the complexity of God's constant action in our lives and our response to it, it is the phrase that Pope Leo and the RCIA employ—"the paschal mystery."

For nearly two thousand years, the Church has never simply taught the paschal mystery. Rather, she has always invited and enabled Christians to participate in that mystery. In response to the challenging question, "What should we ask of catechumens?" the Christian community has followed a basic principle, "the law of worship is the law of belief" (*lex orandi lex credendi*). The paschal mystery is, above all, a continuing, redemptive experience that can only be understood and responded to in the actions and words of praise, thanksgiving, confession, and wonder. What we believe as Christians has always originated in God's action among us.

This chapter examines some of the ways in which the reception of the paschal mystery by Christian communities is tested in the catechumenal process. The challenge of initiation includes questions linked to the Church's experience of the paschal mystery. What ministries in the Christian community help both catechumens and the baptized to participate in the paschal mystery? Is the liturgical year a viable and relevant way, in the twentieth century, of celebrating and responding to the paschal mystery? How do the catechumenal rituals of exorcism and anointing strengthen us to love the paschal mystery?

The Enablers

None of us ever forgets the names of gifted teachers in our lives. These teachers awakened in us the ability to wonder and to experience, and the joy in searching and finding. Creative teachers are not always those with the most advanced academic certification, but they have a fresh and contagious enthusiasm for the process of learning that evokes a similar response in their students.

The history of catechumenal initiation has a list of gifted teachers that includes Tertullian, Origen, Cyril of Jerusalem, John Chrysostom, Ambrose, and Augustine. For each famous name on this list, there are many other anonymous but gifted men and women who once taught others to walk with Christ. Paul's constant reference to his co-workers and to specific house-churches is but one example of such teachers.

When Paul, for example, treats the role of prophets who teach in the community, he lays down one test for their performance—"the upbuilding of the church" (1 Cor. 14:5; also 14:12). The writer of the later Pastoral letters insists on good teaching ability in the leaders of the community (1 Tim. 3:2) and the vital connection between sound teaching and a gospel life (2 Tim. 3:10–11). As in Paul's time, irresponsible and divisive teachers are easily spotted as "empty talkers and deceivers" (Tit. 1:10).

In a series of evocative images, Cyril of Jerusalem, speaking to his fourth-century catechumens, sketches the role of catechumenal teaching and formation as that of a doorkeeper who leaves the door unlocked so that others may enter.[2] Later, he returns to this theme: "Consider it to be the planting season; unless we dig, and that deeply, how shall that afterwards be planted rightly, which has once been planted ill? Or consider catechizing to be a kind of building: unless we dig deep and long the foundation. . . . In like manner we are bringing to thee the stones, as it were of knowledge."[3]

Finally, Origen, the third-century theologian and director of the catechumens, reminds us of what makes great teachers: they model the attitudes to which they invite their students: "I say this for my own correction, not just for that of my listeners. *For I am of those who hear the word of God.*"[4] When reading the names of famous but distant figures, like Origen or Ambrose, we can forget why they had such an impact on their Christian contemporaries: they were not only brilliant theologians but lived what they taught others.

The Catechumenal Team

Paul gives us an apt image to begin our discussion of the ministries that help form and renew Christians. In the first letter to the

Corinthians, the apostle is trying to show the unity of the Christian community, and consequently, the interdependence of gifts of ministry: "You, then, are the body of Christ. Every one of you is a member of it. . . . Are all apostles? Are all prophets? Are all teachers?" (1 Cor. 12:27, 29). As noted above, Paul expects all the authentic gifts and ministries of Christians to build up the community. It is important to remember that Paul is addressing these convictions to a community that is divided and whose ministries do not always build up the Church. Once again, Paul's theology is geared to a praxis-situation that must be changed.

When the Word of God is proclaimed and welcomed, communities of Christians are called together, not to keep the Gospel a secret, but to proclaim it to others. Pope Paul VI in 1975 reiterated that traditional (but sometimes ignored) teaching in his encyclical on evangelization.[5] Both the formation and the renewal of Christians along with the requisite ministries for this task are tied to evangelization, that is, proclamation of the Good News and its implications for our lives. If we ignore evangelization as the starting point for a discussion of how to share the ministries of catechumenal formation, then we reduce the question of becoming Christian to organizational items such as what books to use and what teaching slots need to be filled.

Evangelization is the unifying characteristic of all the ministries involved in the formation of a Christian. The bishop as leader of the local church has the overall responsibility, as did Cyprian, Ambrose, Augustine, John Chrysostom, and so on, before him, to ensure the ecclesial awareness, unity, and sense of mission is his diocese (RCIA, par. 44). To underline this central role, the RCIA names the bishop or his delegate as the ordinary celebrants of the rite of election of candidates considered ready for baptism (RCIA, par. 138). Priests, deacons, and catechists are also part of the catechumenal team (RCIA, pars. 45–48). Above all, the Christian community must understand that the initiation is "the business of all the baptized" (RCIA, par. 41). (On a practical level, the larger community may fulfill this ministry principally on a liturgical level as we shall see later in this chapter.)

There are several theological criteria that apply to anyone who teaches us "the way" and who might be part of the catechumenal team. First, as were Paul, Origen, and Ambrose, they must be "hearers of the Word." There are people who never "miss Mass," but do not hear the Word of God. There are also good-living, nonpractising Christians who may be hearing that Word better than church-goers. A famous example may clarify the point. Augustine, while still a nominal, nonpractising catechumen, began to go to listen to Ambrose preach at Milan, ostensibly to improve his speaking skills. But as Augustine admits, the Word of God in Ambrose's mouth began to trouble the sinful life of the young man.[6] To a superficial observer, however, Augustine would have probably appeared to be someone deaf to the Word of God.

To be an honest hearer of God's Word also entails being a doer of that Word. But some of the potentially best teachers of "the way" may not be the most obvious Christians. Sometimes, Christians have only begun to hear the Word when they are asked to live that Word. An example in our own time is the Young Christian Worker movement in Europe. Often enough, young, nonpractising workers began to listen to God's Word only when they were invited to minister, that is, to concern themselves with the need of their fellow-workers.

Second, a teacher of "the way" must be willing to pray with others who share in the ministries of the catechumenate. (We will develop this point later in the chapter when speaking about the liturgical year.) Although this criterion might seem fairly obvious, in pastoral praxis it is not. There are certain types of liturgical "participation" that seem to allow Christians to escape from any form of shared, more spontaneous prayer with other Christians. Such Christians are at home only with fixed forms of prayer within a controlled and impersonal situation. This limited experience of prayer will hinder such a Christian both from building up a core catechumenal community and from modeling and participating in the rich tradition of Christian prayer with catechumens.

Third, the Christian teacher is willing to struggle with the meaning of God in their own experience. The sense of wonder and thanksgiving in Christian teachers is rooted in the discovery of how God, in Christ, has accompanied them on their own walk to Emmaus. The central teachings of the Gospel are never remote from human experience. Like Paul or Augustine, Teresa of Avila or

Thérèse of Lisieux, Christian teachers are renewed by the effort to see God's paschal mystery patterned in the fabric of their own lives. In this pedagogical model, catechumenal teachers must be more than a source of theological information. They must assist the catechumens to be pathfinders in the often unfamiliar terrain of their own experience. Without this ability, candidates will never appreciate their own need for redemption or the gifts they have been given for ministry to others.

If reviewed more closely, these three criteria for teachers of "the way" concretize the paschal mystery in the lives of a Christian community. The paschal mystery, as a life-long experience of the death and resurrection of Christ, is heard in the Word of God as ever new. The paschal mystery provides the only space and time that can be called sacred for the shared and private prayer of Christians. The paschal mystery is revelatory of our need for God's redemption within the familiar contours of our experience.

These criteria, however, presuppose a certain model of Christian community. If the local parish community operates exclusively around the ordained ministries, whether they be authoritarian or benevolent, the Pauline model of participation of all Christians in the work of the Gospel remains a mystery. Paul himself certainly respected the special ministries within the Christian community, but he was also convinced that these ministries should invite and enable the complementary ministry of all Christians. In praxis, the RCIA cannot operate in an ecclesial vacuum in which the Word of God is liturgically read, but not shared, where liturgical prayer does not serve as a model and incentive for other forms of prayer, and where the ordained ministries have little or not concern for God's action in the lives of his people. Organizational models of community, in praxis, can easily function without the need for these catechumenal criteria, but ecclesial models of community cannot. The catechumenal team, as a microcosm of the ministering Church, need not represent a perfect Christian community, but it must be able to model the results of the paschal mystery as the honest hearing of God's Word, shared prayer, and an awareness of God's action in the lives of both catechumens and the baptized.

The Sponsor's Walk

''Sponsor'' in correct usage refers to someone who underwrites an event or who pays for the advertisement of a product. There is another meaning for sponsor, however, which reflects the Latin origin of the word—someone who is a pledge for another person (*spondere*). An important and ancient ministry within the Christian ministry is that of the catechumenal sponsor who guarantees the changed life-style and sincerity of someone interested in becoming Christian. In the third-century Christian community of Hippolytus at Rome, for example, there is already a requirement that a Christian who knows the candidate vouch for his or her serious intent.[7] In the fourth century, the pilgrim Egeria describes a similar ministry at Jerusalem in which the sponsors are termed ''fathers'' and ''mothers'' of the candidates.[8] During these centuries, the ministry of sponsor also included the practical help and role-modeling that any catechumen would require in a difficult period of transition.[9]

John Chrysostom, a famous catechumenal leader of the fourth century, spells out the role of the sponsor more completely than do most of his contemporaries. He points out that the sponsor accepts the same risk and responsibility as guarantors for money borrowed by someone else.[10] As in the church of Jerusalem, John Chrysostom regards sponsors as spiritual parents who ''show vigilance, advising, counselling, correcting with a paternal affection.''[11] As parents, they assume the privileged duty to guide and teach their children.[12]

In the RCIA, the original role of the sponsor is recognized—that of a friend who ''knows the candidate, helps him, witnesses to his morals, faith, and intention'' (RCIA, par. 42). If this same person, delegated by the local community, continues to be an understanding and helpful companion in the ensuing stages of the catechumenate, he or she is called a godparent. The description of his ministry in the initiation process is, in a real sense, a sketch of a committed Christian: to witness to the Gospel and its implementation in twentieth-century living, to be sensitive to the personal difficulties involved in any true conversion, and to assist the catechumen (and later, the fully initiated person) to welcome and be faithful to the commitment that the paschal mystery demands (RCIA, par. 43).[13]

The experience of being a sponsor/godparent in the catechumenal process has been a turning point in the lives of many Christians who had previously been nominal in their religious commitment and praxis. To fulfill their role honestly, sponsors must be willing, like other catechumenal ministers, to hear God's Word more responsibly, to pray more faithfully, and to reexamine God's action in their own experience. Another factor is the effect of the catechumen's search for God on their baptized companion. The ritual of dismissal of catechumens after the liturgy of the Word on Sunday can have a startling effect on blasé or indifferent Christians. So too can the sincere efforts of a catechumen who does not take for granted what God does among us.[14]

When the ritual of election for candidates ready to enter the final stages of preparation for initiation takes place, it is the godparents who are asked the crucial questions about the commitment of their charges. "Have they faithfully listened to the word of God proclaimed by the Church? Have they been true to the word they have received and begun to walk in God's presence? Have they sought the fellowship of their bothers and sisters and joined with them in prayer? As God is your witness, do you consider these candidates worthy to be admitted to the sacraments of Christian initiation?" (RCIA, par. 144). None of these questions can be honestly answered except by a sensitive and ministering Christian who walks with the catechumen toward the light of the paschal mystery. In brief, all catechumenal ministries nurture and renew the baptized community as they enable the catechumens to celebrate their first Easter. These ministries integrate the liturgical, the doctrinal, and the pastoral dimensions of Christian conversion into a shared and focused experience.[15]

Worship and a Sense of Time

The paschal mystery as participation in the dying and rising with Christ has always marked the Christian sense of time in a unique way. When Luke begins his narration of the resurrection with the words, "On the first day of the week, at dawn" (Luke 24:1), he transposes the notion of this nonsacred, nonsabbath time to a new and redemptive meaning.[16] The effort to become Christian, after all, is worked out, not in some anonymous, Greenwich-mean-time system, but in periods of time shaped by the complex and ever changing experience of our lives. But if Christ is the alpha and omega, the beginning and the end of reality and time, then the would-be Christian must learn to tell time in a different way.

Simon de Vries has cogently argued that in the Word of God there is a unique, qualitative sense of time that marks "a succession of essentially unique, incommensurate experiences."[17] Because God is constantly inviting covenant presence and commitment from his people, these events do not easily permit the Jew to reduce a time to a measure of motion, but rather, to invite a sharing in God's vision for his creation. On the other hand, there is the constant temptation to use worship as a way of "controlling" God and leveling time to a form of measurement. This is a subtle way of avoiding God's message about the end of time and his Kingdom.

In the opening book of the Bible, God's creation of reality is pictured in terms of time, a week of days on the last of which he rests (Gen. 2:3). This seventh day eventually becomes the Sabbath. Later, the rabbis begin to speak of God's Kingdom as the "world which is entirely sabbath."[18] In brief, there is a gradual development of a theology of time which is colored by the idea of how God "works" and "rests" in the days of the Genesis account.

In the New Testament accounts we see how a misconstrued sense of time, work, and rest becomes a major point of contention between Jesus and the Pharisees. The Pharisees taught a theology of strict rest on the sabbath, but certain actions of Jesus seemed to contradict their theology.[19] Matthew in the twelfth chapter of his gospel brings together some of these actions that so infuriated the critics of Jesus. When his hungry disciples begin to pluck grain on the sabbath, for example, the Pharisees protest to Jesus. Then he cures the man with a shriveled hand on the same day. This is his response to his own question, "Is it lawful to work a cure on the sabbath?" (Matt. 12:10).

Behind this debate between Jesus and Pharisees there is the persistent question: why does God give us time? What does it mean to work, and to rest on the "days" of our own genesis story of creation? Jesus contends that the Pharisees have not only perverted the meaning of the sabbath as a day of worship and rest; they have also forgotten the purpose of sacred time: "The sabbath was made for man, not man for the sabbath. That is why the son of Man is lord even of the sabbath" (Mark. 2:27–28). In other words, the sabbath is the gift of a loving Creator—all the more reason, therefore, to remember that love is the proper response and accurate test of our gratitude for this gift of time.[20] Jesus, in the very act of messianic healing on the sabbath shows his concern for the marginal and despised people. In doing this, he sums up key ideas of the Scriptures on the sabbath and renews our sense of the purpose of time.

First, Israel was told to "remember" God on the sabbath because of his covenant love which rescued them from the slavery of Egypt (Deut. 5:15). As Brevard Childs has noted, this is the heart of the sabbath observance in the mind of the writer of the book of Deuteronomy: "Israel observes the sabbath *in order* to remember her slavery and deliverance. . . . The festival arouses and incites the memory. . . . Memory has a critical function of properly relating the present with the past. . . . When Israel observes the Sabbath in order to remember the events of her redemption, *she is participating again in the Exodus event.*"[21]

In other words, the call to worship and rest is also an invitation to participation in a covenant sense of time as redemptive. In contrast to a purely legalistic understanding of the purpose of the sabbath rest and worship, Jesus restores a sense of God's saving action in time by the acts of healing done on that day. In a profound sense, these acts of healing are similar to the prophetic action-words of the Old Testament in which God's dynamic meanings and purpose were revealed to a people who had lost their covenant way. As Jesus' words in Mark emphasize, God does not need our sabbaths; we need them in order to participate in and welcome his saving actions which cut through our dulled sense of time.

Second, in the sabbath debate between Jesus and the Pharisees, another complementary scriptural insight about time is recovered: *to "remember" what God has done for us evokes a cry of praise and acknowledgement that renews our own use of time.* A very complex and nuanced word in Hebrew sums up this theology of praise, thanksgiving, and sacrifice—*todah*.[22] God's constant intrusion into the history of Israel is narrated in order to evoke a renewed faith in his faithful covenant love. As Harvey Guthrie Jr. points out, there is a common method of doing theology which the different writers of the first books of the Bible share—an interpretation of God's actions that evokes worship of thanksgiving, of *todah*. When the creation is described as seven days and the sabbath's meaning is based on the seventh of those days, the overriding response must be one of unbounded gratitude and thanksgiving that deepens our covenant commitment.[23]

The Times of Our Life

A major challenge and test of Christian initiation is a radically new sense of time. Without this awareness of time, we will not praise and thank God as a covenant people. Many of Jesus' contemporaries seem to have lost the connection between their worship and their sense of time. Jesus contested an abstract approach to worship that permitted people to separate their time from God's gift of time. When Jesus healed on the sabbath, he retrieved the covenant idea that time, as part of creation is God's unearned gift. *To share in God's time is to recognize his saving action in our time and to cry out to him with a thankfulness that words can only hint at.*

The Christian church eventually privileged Sunday as the new sabbath of the new covenant. The fascinating and complex historical debate over the origins and dates of this development need not concern us here.[24] Cyril Vogel provides the needed historical summary of how sacred time developed in the Christian church: "The Christian community knew the sanctification of the week before the liturgical year, and the sanctification of Sunday before the feast of Easter."[25] If contemporary Christians or catechumens are to participate in this sanctification of time, they must be able to assess critically their own sense of time as Christian, or perhaps, as still pagan.

Our sense of time is shaped within the specific stages of life that we are experiencing.[26] When we were young, time seemed endless: on a rainy winter day or a hot summer afternoon, "time could hang heavy on our hands," as the popular saying has it. One of the surprising discoveries of life-stage studies in the last two decades is how early in life we begin to sense that "time is running out," that we will not have the time to do all that we wish to accomplish. In brief, time itself becomes a limit-experience. Like all such experiences, these limitations can enable us to be more resourceful and creative with our time or to become paralyzed and dulled in our use of it.

After another week of living, Christians bring to their liturgical praise of God on Sunday whatever sense of time they have salvaged from their lived experience. The pressures of professional life, of dull or routine work situations, of familial or interpersonal tensions and crises can dull, if not warp, our awareness that God's creation as experienced in time is sheer gift. Once this occurs, a legalistic or unreflected approach to worship cannot be far behind.

The symptom of this dulled perception of time as the arena of God's saving action is the complaint of repetition. Young people, for example, sometimes protest against the repetitive nature of Sunday eucharist. And yet, the same people might never think of complaining about the "repetitive" character of being with friends, playing or looking at football, or making love. Repetition, understood as mechanical and meaningless actions, is always framed by an unaware, and often, ungrateful sense of time as a gift with a purpose.[27] When liturgy or worship is repeated within the context of a growing awareness of what God has done and is doing in our lives, then new meaning colors familiar actions and words, and we touch the core of sanctified time: we participate and there is *todah* on our lips and in our hearts.

If the reader reviews how the theology of the Cross (chapter 1) and the Word of God (chapter 2) conspire to help us be honest in our choices and decisions, then their relation to the sanctification of time should already be evident. There is no Christian worship that is not marked by the Cross and shaped by the Word of God. When the Word of God recounts what God has done for us in the crucified and now risen Christ, the purpose of time for the Christian is revealed. First, we have been given once again the gift of time in order, not simply to observe, but to participate in God's work. Second, we are provided with a sacred space and time within which we proclaim a grateful recognition of God's covenant faithfulness. This is indeed repetition, but of the most necessary kind.[28]

There is one word by which the Christian community is tested in its theology of time—"today." The word "today" marks time, but each of us uses the word with our own meanings and values. In the letter to the Hebrews, the writer is not concerned with the Christian community's rituals of liturgy, but with the quality of conversion and commitment that accompanies them. In two successive chapters (Heb. 3–4), he repeats three times the words of Psalm 95: "*Today*, if you should hear his voice, harden not your hearts." The psalm proceeds to narrate how the Israelites had seen God's works for forty years, but had not really changed their attitudes or ways. The writer's first point is about the use of time as God's opportunity: "Encourage one another daily while it is still 'today,' so that no one grows hardened by the deceit of sin" (Heb. 3:13). He restates the psalm's reminder: some people wasted forty years of God's time and did not change.

The writer then modulates to a related theme in Psalm 95: "They shall never enter into my *rest*." He links "rest" with the seventh day of the creation account in Genesis. As A. J. Lincoln points out, Psalm 95 is a liturgical hymn, inviting people to worship and, at the same time, warning them to learn from the wilderness experience of their ancestors who did not honestly worship God. The older meaning of "rest" in Psalm 95, therefore, refers to God's resting place in the temple or sanctuary. But by the time of the letter to the Hebrews, "rest" has also become linked to God's Kingdom and the end of time.[29] The "rest" of the new covenant people is the Kingdom of God: "Therefore a sabbath rest still remains for the people of God. And he who enters into God's rest, rests from his own work as God did from his. Let us strive to enter into that rest, so that no one may fall, in imitation of Israel's example" (Heb. 4:9–11).

In other words, "today" and "rest" chart the Christian's use of time. Against the liturgical background of Psalm 95, the writer is trying to urge Christians in danger of apostasy to see the work of God in their midst and thus, distinguish themselves from the Israelites in the wilderness. The urgency of "today" is matched by the promise of God's "rest" for which the sabbath is a symbol. When God "works" among us, we experience in faith the beginning of his "rest"—the Kingdom.

If the reader feels that we have diverged from our discussion of the challenge of initiation, consider the twentieth-century person's attitude to time and rest. The "Thank God it's Friday" attitude is a logical result of a postindustrial society in which the pressures of scheduling and performance often displace a sense of real time and our decisions about its best use. Bus schedules, appointment books, and entertainment guides substitute for God's "today," which symbolizes the decision to turn to God.[30] Sacred and sanctified time is the combination of what God does and how we respond.

The same society that seems to rob us of a real sense of time can also destroy our sense of "rest." Leisure is an important element in the art of being human, but this is not the meaning of the scriptural term "rest." To abstain from doing the laundry on Sunday, moreover, is not necessarily to understand "a sabbath rest still remains for the people of God" (Heb. 4:9). After all, Jesus defends his conduct on the sabbath against his critics with the words: "My Father works until now, and I am at work as well" (John 5:17).[31] Put another way, we shall not enter God's rest, if he is not at work even "until now."

The paschal mystery is experienced in time. The obstacle to welcoming that mystery, often enough, is our devalued sense of time. To be formed as a Christian implies a renewed outlook on the purpose of time that we have remaining to us. Conversion entails a willingness to respond to God's work in the successive "todays" of our life, and to allow the promise of God's "rest" to alter the ways we work until he comes again. A major help in doing this is the participation of both catechumens and baptized in the liturgical year.

The Liturgical Year

There are families accustomed to setting their clock ahead so that they can be "on time." In fact, groups of people create their own sense of time, for better or worse. The Christian community tries to measure the present time in view of God's future. When the Church celebrates the paschal mystery of Christ's dying and rising, she is not searching for some static historical "replay" of an event, as if it were old newsreel film capturing Good Friday and Easter

Sunday. As already indicated, the biblical sense of time and celebration is linked to participation in and actualization of God's saving action in our midst.

Two of the expressed goals of the catechumenal celebrations of the Word of God are "to explain the signs, actions, and seasons of the liturgy to the catechumens" and "to lead them gradually into the work of the whole community" (RCIA, par. 106,c,d,). The pastoral question suggested early in this chapter is whether the liturgical year remains a relevant way of celebrating the paschal mystery in the twentieth century. We have already begun to answer that question in discussing the Christian sense of time. There is much in our cultural and social background that devalues our sense of sacred time and its celebration. There are also ways of gathering in worship that block out God's test of time—his Kingdom. If a Christian community wishes to symbolize in time the healing and enabling power of God in Christ, then it must learn to love a mystery.

The paschal event, that is, Christ's death and resurrection, is called a mystery with good reason. It is mystery that sanctifies time for the Christian, and gives meaning to the liturgical year, especially in its celebration of Sunday and the feast of Easter. Unfortunately, the word "mystery" in English usually connotes something puzzling or elusive. Even the Greek root of the word (*muein*) with its meaning of "being closed" might deceive us about the Christian usage.[32] Ultimately, mystery opens the door to God's reality.

Mystery is not, first of all, something we know, but an event we experience. For both the catechumen and the baptized a mystery as an experienced encounter is at the core of being Christian. No one knows this better than Paul. Within the body of Pauline writings, we find the term "mystery" used in both a negative and positive sense. In the eleventh chapter of his letter to the Roman Christians, for example, Paul takes up the troubling question about whether God has rejected his own people, the Jews. For Paul, this problem, which he terms a mystery (Rom. 11:25), is but one example of our ignorance of God's ways: "How deep are the riches and the wisdom and the knowledge of God! How inscrutable his judgments, how unsearchable his ways!" (Rom. 11:33).[33] In fact, the beginning of conversion always brings a belated awareness that God does not "think" in the way we do. This is the negative dimension of our encounter with mystery.

On the other hand, Paul believes that the proclamation of the Word of God tears asunder the veil of the Old Testament temple that hides God's mystery: "the gospel which I proclaim when I preach Jesus Christ, the gospel which reveals the mystery hidden from many ages" (Rom. 16:25). When the writer of Colossians speaks of the mystery of God revealed, it is synonymous for him with Christ (Col. 2:2). The "mystery of Christ" (Col. 4:3) is the dynamic experience of God's will to save us. Furthermore, this mystery explains the meaning of time because Christ is linked with God's "fullness of time," that is, when God's plan for his new creation will prevail (Eph. 1:9–10).[34] *In brief, God's mystery is an experience of our ignorance, and God's view of our need and his response. God's mystery challenges our limited awareness of the purpose of time and initiates us into a "time that is not a time and space that is not a space."*[35]

God's mystery for Paul is not a vague and secretive experience that a participant in the Greek religious mysteries of the first century might entertain. The Cross of Christ focuses sharply the mystery of God and leads to the gift of justification without which we could never enter into or love that mystery.[36] For the moment, it is enough to say that justification, as the doorway to the Christian experience, enables us to welcome God's paschal mystery and, like Paul, to perceive a crucified and risen Lord as the ultimate wisdom for our own living and dying. (We will treat justification in more detail in chapter 5.)

In the first of the typical prayers of blessing said over the catechumens at the end of the liturgy of the Word, the celebrant asks: "Lord, may these catechumens come to know the mysteries of your love, be born again in the waters of baptism, and be counted among the members of your church" (RCIA, par. 121). The liturgical year marks out the formation of catechumens and the reeducation of the baptized in coming to know the mysteries of God's love. Authentic participation in that year brings with it the renewed sense of time.

Is Your Time Liturgical?

Josef Jungmann, a great historian of the liturgy, summed up the higher theological purpose of the liturgical year, as "the discernment of what is an essential possession in religious life, and what the passing fashion of an age."[37] To become Christian is to discern what really matters before time runs out. The celebration of the liturgical year, if correctly understood and participated in, is like a good teacher who knows how to focus the attention of the student on what is essential and to point out how the context assists in understanding the texts. In short, the axiom, "the law of worship is the law of belief," is experienced in the shared life of worship within the Church community.

First of all, the liturgical year celebrates and reveals the implicit christologies, for better or worse, of the community. Christology is the systematic study of who Christ is. In addition to these theoretical statements, there is a question of what our actual praxis says about who we think Christ is. Jungmann gives an historical example of this principle. The Arians were heretics who denied the divine nature of Christ. A liturgical way of expressing this heresy was to suppress the ancient conclusion of prayers, "through Christ our Lord." In doing this, they wiped out the redemptive role of Christ in our behalf.[38] The orthodox response was, of course, to reemphasize liturgically that Christ is human and divine.

But an implicit christology also refers to the ways in which people can make correct statements about Christ, but their liturgical actions reveal a quite different idea about him. Paul, for example, perceives that under the orthodox creeds and liturgies of the Corinthian community, there is a mistaken notion about salvation. This implicit christology is exposed, in part, by the insensitive attitudes of some rich Christians toward their poorer brothers and sisters: "When you assemble it is not to eat the Lord's Supper, for everyone is in haste to eat his own supper . . . Would you show contempt for the church of God, and embarrass those who have nothing?" (1 Cor. 11:20–22). In a similar way, a Sunday celebration of the eucharist in the twentieth century can reveal self-serving and comfortable ideas about Jesus as Savior that relieve the community or individual

Christians from sharing in his self-gift and service. These attitudes may betray themselves, for example, in the unwillingness of a parish to deal with the practical corollaries of the Gospel—the ethical questions of nuclear disarmament or unfair housing practices against the poor.

The paschal mystery, as celebrated in the liturgical year, enables us to learn how to pray with honesty and commitment. The catechumen and the baptized experience who Christ is long before they can repeat theological statements about him. Our deep need for a savior is symbolized time and again in the actions and words of worship. For two thousand years, the Church has learned to clarify her christology in her honest praise of Christ.

The liturgical year also celebrates the saving and empowering action of God in the midst of his people: what we celebrate continues in the mission of the Church. What a paradox it would be if a Christian community ritualized this paschal mystery and then did nothing about it. This is a variation on the theme that Jesus states so pointedly: "A man who listens to God's word but does not put it into practice is like a man who looks into a mirror at the face he is born with: he looks at himself, then goes off and promptly forgets what he looked like" (James 1:23–24).

The liturgical year's celebration of what Christ does among us also renews the celebrating community's sense of mission and purpose, if, as the American bishops noted, "we mean the words and want to do what is done."[39] The bishops then add: "To celebrate the liturgy means to do the action or perform the sign in such a way that the full meaning and impact shine forth in clear and compelling fashion."[40] Paul, in effect, sketches the results of honest celebration of God's full meaning: "Every time, then, you eat this bread and drink this cup, you proclaim the death of the Lord until he comes" (1 Cor. 11:26). Paul is not describing effective ritual, but rather the way in which the mystery of God pushes us into participation in it. The mission of the Christian community, both for catechumens and baptized, is the result of "owning" the meanings that we celebrate.

Finally, we can say that a catechumen would never become a Christian, in the deepest sense of the word, without the continuing instruction of the liturgical year in God's mystery. *For liturgy proclaims God's paschal mystery and our entering into that mystery continually and willingly.* "Burn-out" in Christians, on the other hand, is always linked to the way in which they are participating in the meaning and strength of the paschal mystery which we celebrate in the liturgical year. Selfish or escapist motives for our participation allow us to elude God's invitation to witness and to serve.

The Sundays of Our Lives

The word "Sunday" is evocative for many people. "Sunday" conjures up images of leisurely brunches or newspaper reading, of football games on television or time to "catch up." But Sunday is also evocative to anyone who would be Christian. It is the day on which we regularly celebrate the meaning of Christ's dying and rising for us.

But there is always the danger that we will forget the very meanings we celebrate. That is why the catechumenal process should renew the Sunday feast for the baptized at the same time that it teaches candidates how to share in the liturgical prayer of the community. *The first characteristic of Sunday is that it is a gathering.* Although "gathering" is a very broad term in English, its use among early Christians was quite specific. The Church gathered as one family to hear the Word of God and to eat the Lord's Supper.[41]

Paul gives a clue to the purpose of these gatherings: "When you assemble, one has a psalm, another some instruction to give, still another a revelation to share. . . . *Let all things be for the building up*" (1 Cor. 14:26). The expression "building up" captures the ideal that Paul has proposed earlier in the letter: ". . . try to be rich in these (gifts) *that build up the church*" (1 Cor. 14:12). The very unity of the Christian community is a witness and measure of God's work. Sin divides, but salvation brings people together. Gathering as a community on Sunday is, then, a powerful symbol of the Kingdom of God where there will be no walls of division.

But Paul is realistic enough to know that a Christian gathering does not occur simply because people take up space in a building together. In his first letter to the Corinthians, he pointedly repeats the reports he has heard of their divisive gatherings (1 Cor. 11:17).

Selfish preoccupations have begun to distort their sharing of prayer and the eucharist. When Paul reiterates his teaching about the unity of the community that shares the eucharist (1 Cor. 10:17), he is well aware that Christians must take responsibility for the unity that God makes possible.

The Christian community that receives candidates must ask itself if the Sunday eucharist as gathering is simply a polite meeting of people who share a religious tradition or a credible symbol of what we look forward to—a shared future with God. That future, the Kingdom of God, is always described as a gathering: "After this I saw before me a huge crowd which no one could count from every nation and race, people and tongue. I stood before the throne and the Lamb" (Rev. 7:9). As we follow the vivid imagery that the writer of the book of Revelation employs, one central idea about the Kingdom emerges: all these people share the worship of Christ, the Lamb, because their worship and commitment on this earth had forged them into a union of will and love.

Second, the celebration of Sunday invites our participation in the mystery of Christ. The catechumenal process centers around the conviction that Christ's self-gift on the Cross is accessible to us. The catechumen learns to look forward to the very sacraments that the initiated may take for granted—baptism, confirmation, and eucharist. The early Church, in struggling with the meaning of Christ's death, celebrated their initiation and eucharist as a bridge over which they could approach this mystery and share in it. As we shall see in the next chapter, Paul seldom speaks of baptism or eucharist without linking it to the experience of entering into the mystery of Christ's death and resurrection.

The Sunday praxis, however, in an average parish may sometimes seem far removed from this kind of participation. Rituals of celebration can either help or hinder us in participating in the continuing experience of Christ as "someone on account of us." In the compressed period of one hour on Sunday, with its many ritual details, it is easy to forget the central task of the praying community—to be like Christ. In our discussion of the Word of god in chapter 2, we argued for the importance of the liturgy of the Word to assist us in being focused and honest in our celebration of the eucharist. The pastoral effort to make the liturgy of the Word more relevant to this paschal mystery of Christ and our responsive participation in it must be a priority in a gathering of Christians.

When, around the year 150, Justin explains to the Roman emperor how Christians baptize candidates and then celebrate the eucharist, he comments on the meaning of Sunday: "The reason why we all assemble on Sunday is that it is the first day: the day on which God transformed darkness and matter and created the world, and the day on which Jesus Christ our Savior rose from the dead."[42] As we already saw, the idea of God's creation and the sabbath observance were inextricably linked.

Justin restates this theme for the new covenant people: *Sunday rekeys creation as Christ's new creation.* The writer of Genesis can see the work of God in creation, much as the Old Testament authors of the psalms could sing of the beauty of God in the bright stars and roaring oceans. But with Christ everything is made new again. Sunday symbolizes this belief of Christians. We will discuss the twentieth-century relevancy of "new creation" in the next chapter. For the moment, it is enough to say that Sunday provided a radically new vision of God's "ordinary" reality, creation. Linked to this experience of looking at the world as God's, there is the redemptive surprise—the baptized person whom Christ calls a "new creation."

Rituals of Strengthening

Exorcism has always had a certain connotation of the bizarre and exotic in the popular imagination. The audience appeal of the film *The Exorcist*, for example, was due, in no small part, to this discreet interest in the personified power of evil. The Church has never taken evil for granted and this realism is shown in two rituals that accompany catechumens on their journey toward initiation.[43] The baptized can also learn a great deal about the realistic demands of being a "new creation" from understanding and participating in the catechumenal exorcisms and blessings.

John Chrysostom explains exorcism to his fourth-century catechumens as the preparatory cleaning of their "house" to welcome the heavenly king.[44] Cyril of Jerusalem uses a similar comparison with his catechumens but he later sounds the central theme of exorcism: "He who calls, is God, and thou art the person called."[45]

Exorcism deals with the enabling power of God, without which we cannot fight the power of evil. But that power is, as Cyril says, God's call to us.

If we wish to appreciate the contemporary relevance of exorcism, we must briefly survey the New Testament view of Jesus as exorcist.[46] In this role, Jesus is always characterized as filled with the "power" of God. When the Pharisees accuse Jesus of expelling demons with the help of the prince of demons, he promptly points out the eschatological meaning of exorcism: "But if it is by the spirit of God that I expel demons, then the reign of God has overtaken you" (Matt. 12:28). Luke presents the seventy-two disciples sent on mission during the lifetime of Jesus as successful exorcists: "Master, even the demons are subject to us in your name" (Luke 10:17). As Jesus' reply indicates, this is a sign of the beginning of God's final victory over Satan.[47]

In brief, Jesus' "power" (a complex term in both the Old and New Testaments) in expelling demons proclaims that God's victory has begun and his promise to his people is even now vindicated. The actions of Jesus against the power of Satan cannot be separated from the biblical notions of healing, forgiveness, and the reign of God that has already begun among us. When the New Testament proclaims a crucified and risen Lord, this is the final stage of God's triumph over the forces of evil. This theme of Christ's exaltation as synonymous with the ultimate defeat of all other "powers and principalities" is the early Church's Easter card to the world: "It is like the strength he showed in raising Christ from the dead and seating him at his right hand in heaven, high above every principality, power, virtue, and denomination, and every name that can be given in this age or in the age to come. He has put all things under Christ's feet and has made him, thus exalted, head of the church which is his body" (Eph. 1:20–23).[48]

Against this background, the opening line of Matthew's account of Christ's command to baptize has its full impact: "All power has been given me" (Matt. 28:18). Unlike Luke's post-Easter accounts, Matthew has this unique appearance of Christ to his eleven disciples and, in place of the ascension, the writer of the first gospel insists on the continuing presence of Christ in the church: "And know that

I am always with you until the end of time'' (Matt. 28:20).[49] These two ideas of ''all power'' and ''with you until'' frame the risen Lord's command, in Matthew's gospel, to baptize. Technically, we call this ''proleptic parousia,'' which simply means that Matthew describes the reign of God as already begun, with its assurance of Christ's power over all evil and of his guaranteed presence in his Church. When that Church baptizes disciples ''in the name of the Father, and the Son, and the Holy Spirit'' (Matt. 28:19), then the forgiveness, healing, and experience of the reign of God continues to be given. Who Christ is (christology) and what we as a baptized Church should be (ecclesiology) are complementary dimensions of Matthew's last chapter.[50]

To see these same connections, the reader has only to turn to another writing of the New Testament, filled with baptismal imagery, the first letter of Peter. Recalling how Noah and his family ''escaped in the ark through the water'' (1 Pet. 3:20), the writer applies this event to baptism: ''You are now saved by a baptism bath which corresponds to this exactly. This baptism is no removal of physical sin, but the pledge to God of an irreproachable conscience through the resurrection of Jesus Christ. He went to heaven and is at God's right hand, with angelic rulers and powers subjected to him'' (1 Pet. 3:21–22).[51] The writer of 1 Peter is intent on encouraging these Christians not to be overcome by suffering, but to see their own initiation as imitation of Christ who has also suffered and now reigns (1 Pet. 2:20–25).

As the Church developed and ritualized the rich and complex meanings of initiation, exorcism began to have an important place. Our purpose here is not to trace this ritual development, but to underline its theological meaning for the whole Christian community, both catechumens and baptized, in the twentieth century.[52] As we saw above, the New Testament provides us with a mosaic of themes that proclaim one message: the Kingdom of God with its healing, forgiveness, and victory over evil is already beginning among us. The RCIA reflects these themes faithfully in its catechumenal exorcisms, which may be repeated throughout the formation of candidates (RCIA, pars. 111–112).

The rite notes the positive thrust of these exorcisms—''to show the catechumens the true nature of the spiritual life as a battle between flesh and spirit, and underlines both the importance of self-denial in order to gain the blessings of the Kingdom of God and the continuing need for God's help" (RCIA, par. 101). This teaching is concretized in the several prayers of exorcism given in the ritual: "Save our brothers and sisters: free them from all evil and the tyranny of the enemy. Take from them the spirit of falsehood, greed, and wickedness. Receive them into your kingdom and open their hearts to understand your gospel" (RCIA, par. 115); "May they work for peace among people, and joyfully endure persecution. May they come to share in your Kingdom and in the forgiveness you promised them" (RCIA, par. 116).[53]

In the early Church the rituals of exorcism might be accompanied by the laying on of hands or by anointing with oil.[54] In the *Apostolic Tradition* of Hippolytus, for example, the catechumen is anointed with oil in these words: May every kind of evil spirit depart from you.[55] In the current RCIA, the catechumen can be anointed with oil several times during the course of their Christian formation (RCIA, par. 128). The blessing of this oil of catechumens stresses the positive purpose of this ritual—to bring them to a deeper understanding of the Gospel and to help them accept the challenge of Christian living (RCIA, par. 131). When the catechumen is anointed, the operative phrase is, "May he strengthen you with his power" (RCIA, par. 130). This is the complementary dimension of exorcism. The power of evil and Satan is overcome precisely because the strengthening presence of the risen Lord becomes part of the life of this Christian.

Most Christians, baptized as infants, have no recollection of these rituals and, more importantly, do not see the meaning or need for exorcism and catechumenal anointing. And yet, for the nominal Christian, trying to deepen his or her faith, as well as the more fervent Christian, these initiation actions are strong reminders of a realistic theology: evil is a power that can only be overcome by the Risen One to whom all other powers are subject. In an age that has become accustomed to evil as a normal part of the televised evening news, these actions of exorcism and anointing teach us our need and strengthen us for the tasks of the Kingdom.

Some Conclusions

The sign of catechumenal success is a renewed love of the mystery of God that, for the Christian, is focused in the paschal mystery. But the baptized must also continue to be measured by that same mystery. If our hearing of the Word of God improves so that we no longer filter out selected teachings of Christ, if our sense of the sacred is shaped by grateful awareness and praise of what God has given us in Christ, and if we see our revealed need within the pages of our own experience, then surely the paschal mystery of Christ's dying and rising among us is more than a theological footnote for us.

What is sometimes forgotten, however, is that the paschal mystery is not the private preserve of the individual Christian. Because Christ's dying and rising is for the salvation of the whole world, the Christian community celebrates this mystery so that she may continue to be the Body of Christ and to do the work of Christ. The paschal mystery, then, is an effective guard against the selfish use of liturgy in all its aspects.

Liturgy provides a sacred space and time framed by the healing presence of God. The recurring Sunday celebration and the periodic feasts of the liturgical year allow us to clarify who Christ is for us. No more than Peter is the Church permitted to respond vaguely, "Some say you are . . . ," for Christ's question remains, "And you, who do you say that I am?" (Matt. 16:15). Honest liturgy is the clarifying response wrung from our shared experience of God's salvation at work among us: "You are the Messiah . . . the Son of the living God!" (Matt. 16:16).

Both catechumens and baptized receive continuing education in this mystery. When we "gather" in Christ's name, we will have much to learn about God's vision for his creation and our participation in it. As good teachers learn from their students, so the baptized learn from the action of God in the lives of the catechumens. Exorcism of the catechumens is an unsettling reminder of how easily the Christian community can become accustomed to radical evil in its many forms and of our continuing need for healing.

The privileged symbols of the paschal mystery have their extended liturgical celebration in the sacraments of initiation celebrated in the Easter Vigil. If the theology of conversion and the Church in mission that forms the background of these celebrations is taken seriously, then there will be less danger of reducing the feast of Easter to vague discussions of resurrection and even more dubious applications. Resurrection has and continues to be an experience of the crucified and risen Lord among us. Easter is a forceful reminder of this crucial fact.

NOTES

1. Pope Leo the Great, *"Paschale festum, quo sacramentum salutis humanae maxime continetur. . . ."* Ep. 121, 1 as cited by M. B. DeSoos, *Le Mystère Liturgique d'après Saint Léon Le Grand* (Münster: Aschendorff, 1958), p. 80. In translating the Latin text I have followed his conclusions about the nuanced usage of Leo (ibid., pp. 81–83).

2. *The Procatechesis*, 4(in Cross's edition, *The Christian Sacraments*, pp. 2–3).

3. Ibid., 11 (*The Christian Sacraments*, p. 7). I follow Cross's translation here (*The Christian Sacraments*, pp. 46–47).

4. H. J. Auf der Maur and J. Waldram, "Illuminatio Verbi Domini" (see chapter 3, n. 32), n. 27, p. 44; for an excellent delineation of Origen as a catechumenal leader, see ibid., pp. 43–44.

5. Paul Paul IV, *Evangelii Nuntiandi*, I, 16. See also H. J. Urbam, "Wort Gottes und Kirchengemeinschaft," *Catholica* 33(1979):278–91.

6. *Confessions*, Book VI.

7. *Tradition Apostolique*, Botte ed., pp. 32–33; 42–43.

8. *Egeria's Travels*, par. 45 in John Wilkinson's edition (London: SPCK, 1971), pp. 143–44; see also, ibid., pp. 61–62.

9. M. Dujarier, *Le parrainage des adultes aux trois premiers siècles de l'Eglise* (Paris: Cerf, 1962); also, his "Sponsorship," *Adult Baptism and the Catechumenate, Concilium* 22 (New York: Paulist, 1967), pp. 45–50.

10. Baptismal Homily II, 15. I have used the translation of E. Yarnold, *The Awe-Inspiring Rites of Initiation: Baptismal Homilies of the Fourth Century* (Middlegreen, Great Britain: St. Paul, 1971), pp. 163–64.

11. Ibid., p. 164.

12. Ibid., 16, p. 164.

13. It is interesting that the RCIA, par. 43, in its discussion of the godparent refers back to the opening statement that "the whole initiation has a paschal character" (RCIA, par. 8).

14. See J. Villaca and M. Dujarier, "The Various Ministries in Christian Initiation," *Becoming a Catholic Christian: A Symposium on Christian Initiation* (New York: Sadlier, 1978), pp. 144–55.

15. See C. Paliard, "The Place of Catechesis in the Catechumenate," *Adult Baptism and the Catechumenate*, pp. 88–94; also, M. A. Fitzsimons "Systematic Catechesis in the RCIA," *The Living Light* 17(1980):321–26.

16. See B. Botte, "Les Dénominations du dimanche dans la Tradition Chrétienne," *Le Dimanche, Lex Orandi 39* (Paris: Cerf, 1965), pp. 7–28; here, pp. 7–8.

17. S. de Vries, "Time in the Bible," *The Times of Celebration, Concilium 142,* D. Power, ed. (New York: Seabury, 1981), pp. 3–13; here, p. 4.

18. See A. T. Lincoln, "Sabbath, Rest and Eschatology in the New Testament," *From Sabbath to the Lord's Day: A Biblical, Historical, and Theological Investigation,* D. A. Carson, ed. (Grand Rapids: Zondervan, 1982), pp. 198–220; here, pp. 199–200.

19. See C. Rowland, "A Summary of Sabbath Observance in Judaism at the Beginning of the Christian Era," *From Sabbath to the Lord's Day,* pp. 44–55, especially pp. 47–51.

20. See J. Gnilka, *Das Evangelium nach Markus,* vol. 1 (Zürich: Benziger, 1978), p. 123.

21. B. Childs, *Memory and Tradition in Israel* (London: SCM Press, 1962), p. 53 (my emphasis).

22. See H. Guthrie, Jr., *Theology as Thanksgiving: From Israel's Psalms to the Church's Eucharist* (New York: Seabury, 1981), pp. 1–30.

23. Ibid., pp. 36–37, 55.

24. There are two basic positions on the question of the historical development of Sunday. The more traditional position would argue that the apostolic church was responsible for this change. For a major exponent of this position, see, W. Rordorf, *Sunday: The History of the Day of Rest and Worship in the Earliest Centuries of the Christian Church* (Philadelphia: Westminster, 1968). The second position argues that the Sunday observance only arose in the second century at Rome; see S. Bacchiocchi, *From Sabbath to Sunday: An Historical Investigation of the Rise of the Sunday Observance* (Rome: Pontifical Gregorian University, 1977).

25. C. Vogel, *Introduction aux sources de l'Histoire du Culte chrétien au Moyen Age* (Spoleto: Centro Italiano di Studi Sull'Alto Medioevo, 1965), p. 264.

26. See Duffy, *Real Presence,* pp. 68–69; p. 81, n. 36.

27. For another approach, see Y. Spiegel, "Erinnern, Widerholen und Durcharbeiten—Therapeutisches Modell und neuer Gottesdienst," *Erinnern—Widerholen—Durcharbeiten: Zur Sozialpsychologie des Gottesdienstes,* Y. Spiegel, ed. (Stuttgart: Kohlhammer, 1972), pp. 9–33.

28. For a different (structuralist) approach, see L-M. Chauvet, *Du Symbolique au Symbole: Essai sur les sacrements* (Paris: Cerf, 1979), pp. 219–35.

29. Lincoln, "Sabbath, Rest and Eschatology in the New Testament" (supra n. 18), pp. 208–10.

30. See, for example, L. Duch, "The Experience and Symbolism of Time," *The Times of Celebration* (supra n. 17), pp. 22–28.

31. See R. Brown, *The Gospel According to John (I–XII)* (Garden City, N.Y.: Doubleday, 1966), pp. 216–17.

32. Dom Odo Casel, a creative Benedictine scholar, is usually credited as having retrieved the importance of the concept of mystery for understanding of liturgy and sacrament. Casel's position has been the center of controversy for some years; see T. Filthaut, *La Théologie des mystères, exposé de la controverse* (Tournai: Desclée, 1954); for a more recent and positive reevaluation, see A. Schilson, *Theologie als Sakramententheologie: Die Mysterientheologie Odo Casels* (Mainz: Matthias-Grünewald, 1982).

33. For the scriptural background of "mystery," see the classic article of G. Bornkamm, *musterion, Theological Dictionary of the New Testament* IV:802–28; also R. E. Brown, "The Semitic Background of the New Testament *Mysterion*," *Biblica* 39(1958):426–48; 40(1959):70–87; idem, "The Pre-Christian Semitic Concept of 'Mystery'," *Catholic Biblical Quarterly* 20(1958):417–43.

34. See Bornkamm's remarks in *musterion*, ibid., 823–24. D. Lührmann has argued persuasively that these "mystery" passages are examples of "revelation-schemata," which teach through antithetic parallelism (such as, hidden/revealed); see his *Das Offenbarungsverständnis bei Paulus und in Paulinischen Gemeinden* (Neukirchen-Vluyn: Neukirchener Verlag, 1965), pp. 124–32; for a possible liturgical dimension in these scriptural citations, see ibid., pp. 132–33.

35. I summarize an idea of Victor Turner's, *communitas*; see my article, "A Test for Communitas: Team Ministry," *Worship* 48(1974):566–79.

36. Lührmann, *Das Offenbarungsverständnis*, pp. 139–53.

37. J. Jungmann, *Pastoral Liturgy* (New York: Herder and Herder, 1962), p. 2.

38. Ibid., pp. 29–32; for other examples, see also, pp. 45, 49.

39. *Music in Catholic Worship*, par. 3.

40. Ibid., par. 7.

41. See Meeks, *The First Urban Christians*, pp. 142–50.

42. The text with commentary can be found in M. Jourjon, "Justin," *The Eucharist of the Early Christians*, R. Johanny, ed. (New York: Pueblo, 1978), pp. 71–85; here, p. 73.

43. The RCIA (par. 111) permits the so-called "minor" exorcisms (as opposed to the exorcisms of the scrutinies just prior to baptism) to begin even during the precatechumenal period of evangelization.

44. Baptismal Homily II, 12 in Yarnold, *The Awe-Inspiring Rites*, p. 162.

45. *The Procatechesis*, 9, in Cross, *Lectures on the Christian Sacraments*, p. 6 (Greek text); p. 46 (English text).

46. For some background, see L. Sabourin, "The Miracles of Jesus (II)," *Biblical Theology Bulletin* 4(1974):115–75 (especially 140–75); P. Achtemeier, "Miracles and the Historical Jesus: Mark 9:14–29," *Catholic Biblical Quarterly* 37(1975):471–91; O. Böcher, *Christus Exorzista: Dämonismus und Taufe im Neuen Testament* (Stuttgart: Kohlhammer, 1972), pp. 166–80.

47. Ibid., p. 168.

48. For similar citations, see Eph. 4:8–10; Phil. 2:9ff.; Col. 2:10, 15; Heb. 2:8, 14.

49. As Meier points out, "For Matthew, the resurrection is the exaltation. There is no separate act of exaltation labeled ascension or 'being taken up', as in Luke" (*The Vision of Matthew*, p. 38, n. 40).

50. Ibid., p. 214.

51. N. Brox, *Der Erste Petrusbrief* (Cologne: Benziger, 1979), pp. 164–82, especially pp. 177–78; F. W. Beare, *The First Epistle of Peter* (Oxford: Blackwell, 1970), pp. 173–74.

52. The classic work here is still F. J. Dölger's *Der Exorzismus im altchristlichen Taufritual: Eine religionsgeschichtliche Studie* (Paderborn: F. Schöningh, 1909). A more recent discussion can be found in G. Kretschmar, "Die Geschichte des Taufgottesdienstes in der alten Kirche," *Leitourgia* 5(1972):1–348; especially 89, 227–228; A. Stenzel, *Die Taufe: Eine genetische Erklärung der Taufliturgie* (Innsbruck: Rauch, 1957), pp.154–57.

53. For a brief comparison of the exorcism of the pre–Vatican II rituals with the current ones, see B. Fischer, ''Baptismal Exorcism in the Catholic Baptismal Rites after Vatican II,'' *Studia Liturgica* 10(1974):48–55; R. Béraudy, ''Scrutinies and Exorcisms,'' *Adult Baptism and the Catechumenate, Concilium 22* (New York: Paulist, 1967), pp. 57–61, though I find the latter's interpretation of exorcism somewhat limited.

54. See Böcher, *Christus Exorcista*, pp. 132, 176 (laying on hands); pp. 100–101 (oil); Kretschmar, ''Die Taufe,'' pp. 89, 95.

55. Par. 21, Botte ed., supra n. 7, p. 47.

Chapter 5

TO LOVE A MYSTERY

Some people maintain that they are honest despite others around them. Authentic Christians feel that they could not be honest without the help of others. The Lenten challenge of initiation can be phrased this way: How do we enable one another to serve again and thus honor our initiation commitment? Christian honesty turns on the baptismal promises that we have made or intend to make— to be like Christ. The practice of Lent arose from questions about the honesty of the Easter feast that Christians celebrated so readily. The continuing temptation of the Christian community is to celebrate the paschal mystery as a stale but reassuring history of salvation. But the celebration of Lent and Easter tests the credibility of our self-description as Christian and asks us if we have forgotten the real reasons for which we still baptize others.

Cyril of Jerusalem in his fourth-century talks to the candidates reminds them that they were called catechumens, that is, people "hearing with the ears, hearing hope, and not perceiving; hearing mysteries, yet not understanding: hearing Scriptures, yet not knowing their depth."[1] But Cyril notes an important change that is now imminent. The catechumens will begin to hear the mystery within their soul because the Spirit has made them into a house of God. Actually, Cyril's catechumenal listeners were a special group. In Jerusalem they were called "those destined for the enlightenment" (*photizomenoi*), while at Rome or Carthage they would be described as "those who were seeking (initiation)" (*competentes*). This group was prepared to complete their preparation for Christian initiation by "handing in their name" (technical term within the catechumenal system for this turning point) on the first Sunday of Lent.

Lent is originally, then, the last phase of catechumenal progress. But, as we shall see, the honesty of one group within the Christian community depends on and challenges the other groups. The baptized, seeing the catechumens' effort to become Christian, were forced to reconsider their own commitment. Lent became a period of reassessment and recommitment. Without the shared learning and encouragement of Lent, Easter would be an impossible feast. But with such feasts in our lives, we learn again the richness of the paschal mystery and why the Church continues to baptize.

The mystery of Easter is at the heart of what we are and do as Christians. But without the catechumenal context of Lent and Easter, these crucial events in the life of the Christian community can be reduced to a privatized piety and some historical mementos. This chapter draws out some of the theological implications of how both catechumens and baptized are reeducated in the paschal mystery during the season of Lent. The amazing ability of the Church to symbolize this mystery is revealed in the rich and ancient traditions of the election of the catechumens, the scrutinies and presentations of Lent, and the ways in which the Pauline theology of initiation is dramatically imaged in rituals of fire, water, and oil of the Easter vigil.

But the question that underlies this whole discussion is whether we Christians love a mystery—the paschal mystery. In our own age of computerized analyses and scientific breakthroughs, the word "mystery" seems to have a limited usage. One thinks of a murder mystery or a temporary puzzle that will eventually be solved. But the Christian sense of God's mystery, revealed in the Easters of our lives, is a limit-experience that clears the vision and unstops the ears. As Cyril indicated, when we hear and see in this way, we will never be the same again.

A Time of Shared Decision

Originally, Ash Wednesday was not the beginning of Lent. By the fourth century at least, it was the custom for catechumens who were ready to enter the proximate preparation for baptism to hand in their name on the first Sunday of Lent. This was a decisive action of commitment in the persecuted churches of the third century. With the official toleration of the Church by the Roman state in the fourth century, it was sometimes advantageous to be a "perpetual catechumen" either for social or professional reasons, or to have two opportunities for forgiveness of sins later in life.[3]

The plaintive urging of bishops like Ambrose and Augustine to their catechumens to "hand in their names" reveals the demanding nature of this ritual and the pastoral problem of dealing with candidates for initiation who sometimes lacked the motives for being Christian.[4] Yet Ambrose and Augustine, as young men, had been, ironically, examples of this same hesitation before their complete commitment to the gospel way.

In the current RCIA, this enrollment of names is also called the rite of election. This process marks a turning point in which catechumens will now be called the "elect" and when the Christian community will "walk" this Lent with them. But the crucial first step of this new stage is the election. As the RCIA indicates clearly, this is not a routine approval of candidates. The criterian for judging the readiness of the catechumens is "an enlightened faith and the deliberate intention of receiving the sacraments of the Church. After the election, he/she is encouraged to advance toward Christ with even greater generosity" (RCIA, par. 134). The previous four chapters of this book are an attempt to spell out some of the implications of an enlightened faith and readiness for the sacraments of initiation.

With this question of election, however, we return to the opening challenge of this book: Does the local community still know why she is receiving candidates for initiation? In the pre–Vatican II church, we easily recall that caricature of religious education—the person who knew all the catechism answers, but had no intention of living them. In the post–Vatican II church, there is still the danger that a relevant theological preparation can be mistaken for an enlightened faith and readiness for honest sacramental celebration. The ritual questions addressed to the godparents reflect the pastoral accountability for the whole Christian community for the preparation of these candidates: "Have they faithfully listened to the Word of God proclaimed by the Church? Have they been true to the word they have received and begun to walk in God's presence? Have they sought the fellowship of their brothers and sisters and joined with them in prayer?'' (RCIA, par. 144).

The seriousness of election and the community's accountability is emphasized in other ways. The bishop (or his delegate) is the normal celebrant of this rite (RCIA, par. 138). At this moment, the bishop follows the example of an illustrious line of catechumenal leaders—Cyprian, Cyril of Jerusalem, John Chrysostom, Ambrose, and Augustine. Several groups within the community must share in the election according to their responsibility: the bishop, priests and deacons, the catechumenal personnel, the godparents, and the community at large (RCIA, par. 135).[5] The responsibility of the godparents is also underlined in an alternative ritual: ''As God is your witness, do you consider these candidates worthy to be admitted to the sacraments of Christian initiation?'' (RCIA, par. 145).

It is not hard to see why the election of the catechumens is described as ''the turning point in the whole catechumenate'' (RCIA, par. 23). The community must review its own Christian praxis and awareness, before it can honestly decide whether a candidate is ready to celebrate fully the paschal mystery. The various ordained and nonordained ministeries in the diocese and the local community are also forced to reassess their pastoral priorities: What response should their work among their fellow Christians evoke? Do the criteria by which candidates are judged (listening and acting on the Word of God and response in prayer) also represent some of the pastoral priorities for working with the baptized? To elect the catechumens, then, is to recommit oneself to the work of the Gospel in the life of the Christian community and of the individual.

In short, the catechumenal program is a potential catalyst for Christian awareness. When Augustine, for example, emphatically states, ''I do not hesitate to put the catholic catechumen, burning with charity, before the baptized heretic. *And even within the bosom of the Catholic church, we prefer the good catechumen to the bad baptized person*,'' we can appreciate how the commitment of the as yet unbaptized catechumen (or the returning Christian) serves as a mirror in which the rest of us can reexamine our own lives.[7] This pastoral effort of stirring up both the practicing and the nonpracticing Christian, the baptized and the catechumen resulted in an annual season of renewal in the Church, Lent.

Lent as Shared Renewal

"Credibility" is derived from the Latin word "to believe" (*credere*), and means literally "believability." In the previous chapters of this book, we have outlined what can change in our world and in our lives because of what God continues to do in Christ. To many people, however, this is pure theory that has nothing to do with the reality of their lives. Whether they are listening to the televised evening news with its constant accounts of war, famine, murder, and rape, or simply assessing the less-than-ideal day they have just lived, there is a problem of credibility in being convinced that the Gospel makes a difference. Even within the Christian community, it is not rare to find mediocrity, if not outright hypocrisy. We could phrase the resulting pastoral question in this way: Are we preparing candidates for a Christian community and mission which does not, in fact, actually exist?

In the pre–Vatican II church, Lent was generally viewed as a period of personal penance. There was always the danger that this season might be misunderstood as some neopelagian exercise of spiritual self-improvement that had little to do with the reasons for God's action in the lives of people, and with the mission of the baptized community, the Church. In practice, Lent had become separated from its origins—the final preparation of the catechumens for initiation and of the baptized who were penitentially recommitting themselves to the gospel way of life.

Even in the third-century documents of Church communities, such as that of the *Apostolic Constitution* of Hippolytus, there is a definite period of time set aside for the proximate preparation of catechumens that precedes the rites of initiation. There are forms of examination and election of the candidates, doctrinal and moral instruction, exorcisms, and days of fasting. Leo the Great sums up this process, by now established as the Lenten season, in a succinct formula: to scrutinize by exorcism, to sanctify by fast, and to inspire with frequent preaching.[8]

Historically, the celebration of Easter had gradually been enlarged to include a three-day period (our Good Friday, Holy Saturday, Easter Sunday) with fasting on the first two days. By the fifth century this triduum had developed into the Holy Week observance.[9] Lent, as the immediate preparation of catechumens chosen for initiation in the upcoming celebration of Easter is already in place in the early fourth century.[10] By the end of the fifth century the familiar Ash Wednesday is the beginning of the Lenten season.

As the Lenten observance developed, the catechumenal character of the season was complemented by a penitential dimension. In fact, there were two groups of penitents among the baptized. The first group consisted of Christians who had entered canonical penance either because of the nature of their sins or out of a desire to do greater penance. Canonical penance, however, is only comprehensible within the catechumenal process and a theology of initiation as commitment to the gospel way.

The early Church proclaimed a baptism for the remission of sin to adults. When the Church was confronted with the flawed commitment of many baptized Christians who continued to sin seriously after their initial forgiveness, the question arose, Can there be a second forgiveness of sins?[11] Canonical penance was the Church's response: once in a lifetime after initiation the Christian might again enter a process of recommitment, similar to the catechumenal process. After a severe and usually prolonged period, the penitent was reconciled during Lent. Some aspects of their penitential life, however, remained with them until their death. *In a real sense, the catechumen saw the penitent as a mirror of his or her own effort to become an honest Christian.* Both catechumen and penitent fasted, were prayed over, and served as a prophetic reminder within the Christian community about the cost of dying and rising with Christ over a lifetime. (In the next chapter we will return to this question of a renewed celebration of reconciliation in the light of the catechumenal model.)

The second group of Lenten penitents was the rest of the Christian community. Catechumenal and canonical penitents embodied the gospel question to the larger community: Have you ceased becoming Christian? This question is a major theme of Christian leaders during these centuries. Augustine, for example, distinguishes the "newness" of the recently baptized and the "healing" of those long baptized.[12] Pope Leo returns often to this same theme in his preaching: "It is characteristic indeed of the paschal celebration that the whole church rejoices in the forgiveness of sins, not only of those who have only just been reborn in sacred baptism, but also of those who have long been numbered among the adopted children (of God).''[13]

In the RCIA, Lent is once again viewed as preparation for baptism and a time for penance: ''It renews the community of the faithful together with the catechumens and makes them ready to celebrate the paschal mystery, which the sacraments of initiation apply to each individual'' (RCIA, par. 21; also, par. 152). Lent is, in effect, a question of Christian credibility. There is no question that Christ's presence in the Church makes all things possible, but there is a serious question about the way in which we, catechumens and baptized, welcome these redemptive possibilities.

When we addressed, in chapter 2, the problems of being a Christian community and maintaining a sense of mission, we argued for the catechumenal process as a renewal of the whole community. Lent is the season for renewing our belief in Christ's presence, and the difference it makes in the community and in the world. Lent provides a realistic focus on the radical sin that still haunts the evening news and our own lives. Christian credibility, which Lent renews, is an echo of the Pauline conviction: ''But despite the increase of sin, grace has far surpassed it, so that, as sin reigned through death, grace may reign by way of justice leading to eternal life through Jesus Christ our Lord'' (Rom. 5:20–21).

Exorcism as Enacted Gospel

In the previous chapter we discussed exorcism as a regular feature of the catechumenal process. But Lent is a season in which the crucial summarizing of the catechumenal experience and knowledge is dramatically symbolized in a series of Sunday rituals of exorcism known as the scrutinies.[14] (The Latin root of ''scrutiny'' means to judge or appreciate.) On the third, fourth, and fifth Sundays of Lent, after the homily and prayers for the elect, the celebrant lays hands on the candidates. The two-fold purpose of this powerful symbol is to heal what is weak and strengthen what is upright (RCIA, par. 25; also, par. 154).

But there are two distinctive features about these solemn exorcisms. First, they are celebrated on Sunday in the presence of the larger Christian community, in contrast to the exorcisms of the catechumenal period. Second, these exorcisms are framed by some of the oldest choices for gospel readings that we know of in series A in the Roman lectionary.[15] The Gospel for the third Sunday is that of the Samaritan woman (John 4:4–42), the fourth Sunday, that of the man born blind (John 9:1–41), and the fifth Sunday, that of the raising of Lazarus (John 11:1–44).

As Rudolf Schnackenburg has reminded us, the Gospel of John deals with the process of believing in a unique way. Summing up the Johannine use of words such as ''to believe,'' ''to reveal,'' and ''to see,'' he says: ''Revelation cannot be fully grasped in a rational manner, but it requires an answer coming from the totality of human behavior and from personal decision ... it touches the very core of his personal being and leads him to a crisis, to the situation of a personal decision.''[16] The complementary aspect of this Johannine treatment of revelation is ''witness.'' The Samaritan woman, the young man born blind, and Lazarus each testify and witness to the fact that Jesus is Savior. But each one comes to this awareness through a process of insight and awakening.

The three Johannine readings graphically summarize the Christian understanding of the process of coming to faith and its result, new life. The Samaritan woman's request for ''living water'' (John 4:15) is a powerful metaphor for the reawakened thirst for the faith of the catechumen. The prayer that precedes the exorcism of the third Sunday of Lent reflects the gospel theme: ''These men and women preparing for baptism thirst for living water as did the Samaritan woman. May the word of God change their lives, too, and help them to acknowledge the sins and weakness that burden them'' (RCIA, par. 164). The gospel theme contextualizes the exorcism and, at the same time, reminds the initiated Christian community of its own continuing need for exorcism.

In the second scrutiny, the prayer before the exorcism again takes up the gospel theme of the fourth Sunday of Lent: ''Grant them to enjoy your light like the man whose sight you once restored and inspire them to become fearless witnesses to the faith'' (RCIA, par.

171).[17] In the fifth Sunday's prayer before the exorcism another related baptismal theme is announced: "Lord Jesus, you raised Lazarus from death as a sign that you had come to give people life in the fullest measure. Rescue from death all who seek life from your sacraments and free them from the power of evil" (RCIA, par. 178). We have quoted extensively from these prayers because it is rare that the Sunday gospels are not only commented on, but then find a nonverbal commentary in a ritual such as exorcism.

What is striking about the exorcisms on these Lenten Sundays of scrutiny is the way in which they mirror the continuing need of the baptized community as well as that of the catechumens. The theological question about the paschal mystery and the pastoral question about the implementation of Lent are clarified in these highly coded rituals of scrutiny. As R. Schnackenburg suggests, the dramatic intensity of the Johannine idea of God's call in his revealed Word and our response in faith challenges our sometimes overly intellectualized and minimally experienced faith.

Lent is a reeducation in how we ought to respond to the paschal mystery. The need for exorcism is a key element in this reeducation. The pressing questions that underlie this rite should be taken seriously: When did we last thirst for the "living water" which is Christ?[18] Does Christ's reproach to the Pharisees who refuse to accept the miracle of the man born blind apply to us: " 'But we see,' you say and your sin remains" (John 9:41)? Has our own keenness for resurrection been so dulled by mediocre Christian living that the Lazarus scene has been reduced to an exegetical footnote?

Scrutiny, then, is an apt description of a process of reevaluation of the Christian community as well as a evaluation of the catechumens. Even if we do not choose to invite the baptized to be exorcized ritually during Lent, we should enable them to review the troubling questions of exorcism that they think have been definitively answered long ago. Perhaps one of the petitions that is offered for the catechumens sums up the need of the unexorcized Christian: "Let us pray for these men and women whom God has chosen, that their lives remain centered in him and they may offer convincing witness to the message of eternal life" (RCIA, par. 169).

"Do Not Pray as the Pagans"

The warning of Ambrose to his catechumens may strike us as somewhat strange: "The creed should not be written down. You have to be able to repeat it, but no one must write it down."[19] At some point, the Church began to protect aspects of her worship and doctrine from the inevitable misunderstandings or scorn of nonchristians.[20] Within the catechumenal process this meant a gradual revelation and explanation of the faith. The rituals of initiation on Holy Saturday seem to have been usually explained after the event. Ambrose says to his newly baptized: "I shall begin now to speak of the *sacraments which you have received*. It was not proper for me to do so before this, because, for the Christian, faith must come first."[21] But there is a good deal of scholarly disagreement as to how much this secrecy was maintained even in the time of Ambrose.[22]

Whether or not secrecy prompted the ritual of "handing over" (*traditio*) and eventually "receiving back" (*redditio*) the Creed and the Our Father, these actions remain one of the most provocative rituals of the current RCIA. The Creed is presented by the celebrant and the community to the catechumens in the week following the first scrutiny (RCIA, par. 184). The Our Father is given after the third scrutiny (RCIA, par. 189). These two prayers, which so easily become monotonous and hackneyed with regular use, assume their original context in these catechumenal rituals of presentation—that of discipleship.

In introducing the Creed, the celebrant says to the catechumen: "The words are few, but the mysteries they contain are awe-inspiring" (RCIA, par. 186). The thought applies equally to the Our Father. Both prayers sum up the whole experience of what God does in our lives. The axiom, "the law of worship is the law of belief," is once again verified. In "handing over" these prayers, the Church teaches the catechumen and reminds the baptized that the experience of God is the root of saving doctrine. In other words, the Church does not simply give us words of belief, but rather, witnesses to God's action in our lives. The Church "hands over" these summaries of belief to people who profess to believe.

Paul connects the words of belief with the faith of the believer: "For if you confess with your lips that Jesus is Lord, and believe in your heart that God raised him from the dead, you will be saved. Faith in the heart leads to justification, confession on the lips to salvation'' (Rom. 10:9–10). ''Jesus is Lord'' is probably a baptismal confession that Paul cites.[23] But it is the faith of the person being baptized that responds and witness to what that Risen Lord has accomplished. While faith is within the person, Paul insists, however, that it must be proclaimed publicly. There are no private creeds for the Christian: faith and its proclamation within a community of faith are inseparable in Paul's mind.

Augustine provides an excellent illustration of these complementary personal and public dimensions of faith in an anecdote that had been told him by Simplicianus, the priest who taught both Ambrose and Augustine. A famous and influential Roman philosopher, Victorinus, became convinced of the truth of Christianity through his secret reading of the Scriptures. On one occasion he privately admitted to Simplicianus that he was a Christian inwardly. Simplicianus insisted that he would not believe this until '' 'I see you in the Church of Christ.' Whereupon he (Victorinus) replied derisively, 'Is it then the walls that make Christians?' ''[24] Eventually Victorinus confronts the dichotomy between his inner faith and his shame of publicly admitting that faith, and is enrolled as a catechumen.

In Augustine's continuing narrative, we have not only a valuable historical and liturgical witness to ''confession on the lips,'' but an implicit theology that connects faith and sacrament: ''Finally, when the hour arrived for him to make profession of his faith (which at Rome they who are about to approach Thy grace are wont to deliver from an elevated place, in view of the faithful people in a set form of words learnt by heart), the presbyters . . . offered Victorinus to make his profession more privately, as the custom was to do those who were likely through bashfulness, to be afraid; but he chose rather to profess his salvation in the presence of the holy assembly. . . . He pronounced the true faith with an excellent boldness, and all desired to take him to their very heart.''[25]

Augustine relates this story as a preface to a perceptive analysis of his own situation: an intellectual conviction about the truth of the Christian faith, but a persistent unwillingness to profess the commitment of faith that would entail a number of practical corollaries in his private and public life. His autobiographical admission to God captures this dilemma: "And to Thee showing me on every side, that what Thou saidst was true, I, convicted by the truth, had nothing at all to reply, but the drawling and drowsy words: "Presently, lo, presently; leave me a little while.' ''[26]

Faith is always a sheer gift, and never tied to our own worthiness or moral performance. When Augustine must defend this traditional teaching of the Church against the Donatists, he insists on the objective presence of Christ in sacrament, which is grounded in the unearned nature of faith and the perduring holiness of the Church as the "body of Christ."[27] Sometimes commentators, however, can forget that Augustine is writing his monograph, *On Baptism*, against the Donatists at the same time as his *Confessions*. These writings represent complementary aspects of the same teaching on faith and sacrament. Only God's unearned love and healing permit flawed Christian communities to be called the "body of Christ" and enable them to respond honestly to God's presence in the proclamation of faith and its celebration in sacrament.

This otherwise abstract discussion is concretized in "handing over" of the profession of faith and the Our Father. In a profound sense, these symbols of faith are words to the music that we already know. *The catechumenal process is an unfolding experience within a community of faith in which we learn to profess gratefully the action of God in Christ in our lives in the words of belief and discipleship.* There is evidence that Christian communities even in the time of Ambrose and Augustine were still using an interrogatory creed that accompanied the baptism of candidates. Cyprian, in fact, terms this liturgical practice "to baptize by means of the creed" (*symbolo baptizare*).[28] (The remnants of this practice are familiar to contemporary Christians in the renewal of baptismal vows on the Easter Vigil.)

Ambrose reminds the newly baptized of the manner in which they received the sacrament of initiation: "You were asked: 'Do you believe in God, the all powerful Father?' You replied: 'I believe,' and you were immerged. . . . A second time you were asked: 'Do you believe in our Lord Jesus Christ and in his cross?' You answered: 'I believe,' and you were immerged. . . . You were asked a third time: 'Do you believe in the Holy Spirit?' You responded: 'I believe,' and you were immersed a third time."[29] These were not rhetorical questions, but rather the public conclusion to a long process or formation in faith.[30]

Long before the initiation of the adult, the first steps of faith should already have been taken. When the RCIA, then, states the traditional teaching of the Church that catechumens are already "joined to the Church and are part of the household of Christ" (RCIA, par. 18), the reason should be evident. The opening paragraph of the RCIA, in describing the catechumenal process, provides an outline of that formation in faith: "They hear the preaching of the mystery of Christ, the Holy Spirit opens their hearts, and they freely and knowingly seek the living God and enter the path of faith and conversion" (RCIA, par. 1).

The "handing over" (and subsequently, "handing back" by the catechumens) of the Creed and the Our Father restores the underlying question of the relation of faith and sacrament to its original context: the gradual catechumenal process of learning to believe in a saving God—Father, Son, and Spirit.[31] When this model is applied to those who consider themselves Christians or who are trying to appropriate a faith that they did not originally seek when baptized as infants, some theological and pastoral reminders about the nature of faith and its celebration in sacrament emerge.[32]

First, God's gift of faith must be actively welcomed. The RCIA notes correctly the sequence of faith: the Word of God and the power of the Spirit enable us to "freely and knowingly seek the living God" (RCIA, par. 1). This sequence is not a description of candidates who feel at the moment of baptism that "they have made it." In contrast to the catechumenal process that does not presume faith but helps the candidate "freely and knowingly seek," some sacramental praxis assumes an active faith on the part of those who ask for a sacrament even when there may be signs to the contrary (nominal Christians, for example, who want to be "married in a church"). The words of the Creed or the Our Father cannot be substituted for the commitment demanded by these texts. If a sacrament is to be honest on the part of the recipient as well as the Christian community, then their faith must reflect, in some way, their free and knowing effort to seek the living God.

The catechumenal process, moreover, is a pastorally realistic guide: each person responds to God's gift of faith out of his or her own unique and flawed experience. There has never been an absolute pastoral norm to assure the Christian community that this particular adult is ready for initiation (or, ready to return to the practice of Christianity). Rather, the Christian community has usually tried to recognize the first steps of faith within the cultural, social, and psychological contexts that can differ widely within the same American city or even family. When we apply this guideline to the pastoral question of how much faith is necessary for the honest and worthy reception of a sacrament (for example, the case of the sacramental marriage of nominal Christians), there is a flexible but demanding norm: Are your words of belief matched in any way in your current life-stage by actions of belief?

The "handing over" of the Creed and the Our Father also suggests a second theological and pastoral reminder: *the Christian community must actively model her preaching, teaching, sacramental praxis, and pastoral care on the catechumenal assumption that faith is a continuing formation in honest professions of faith and challenging sacrament.* One test of this model is the way in which catechumens and the baptized, practicing and nominal Christians, become aware of the need to do the work of the Gospel if the words of the Gospel are to come alive. In brief, the saving actions of God recounted in the Creed, and the disciple-plea of "Thy Kingdom come" in the Our Father are actualized in the mission of the Church in each historical epoch. The proof of this contention is the celebration of the liturgical year within the Christian community, which praises God not only for what he did long ago but what he is currently doing in our world and in our midst. Our participation in God's continuing "new creation" among us is expressed in a petition for the elect, after the handing over of the Our Father— "that God in his mercy make them responsive to his love" (RCIA, par. 192).

The Night of Nights

Augustine describes the Easter Vigil, with good reason, as "the most sweet of feasts."[33] In a highly condensed process of symbolization, the Easter Vigil sums up the whole paschal mystery, as it comments on the human response to that mystery in its celebration of initiation. The Easter Vigil is the proper time for the initiation of adults (RCIA, pars. 8, 208). Even if initiation is celebrated outside this time, it should be "filled with the Easter spirit" (RCIA, par. 209). But what is that spirit?

We do not know when and where the original liturgical praxis of initiating the elect into the Church on the Easter Vigil began.[34] By the third century, however, we find Tertullian's description of Easter as a more proper time for baptism "when the passion of Christ in which we were baptized was fulfilled."[35] Our limited purpose in the rest of this chapter is to appreciate the theology of initiation as celebrated on that night of nights. Before commenting, however, on the meaning of such rituals as the renunciation of Satan, water baptism, and anointing with chrism, it is important to return to the theologian who bridges the Cross and the resurrection of Jesus with our own initiation experience—the Apostle Paul.

Long before there was an annual feast of Easter, Paul brilliantly captured the essence of initiation as becoming like Christ.[36] Just as the Easter Vigil celebration of initiation sums up the lengthy process of conversion, so the teaching of Paul on baptism must always be seen against the larger background of his treatment of the conversion that justification makes possible.

We began this book with a discussion of Paul's insistence on the importance of the Cross. Everything which the Christian receives can be traced back to Christ's self-gift. In practical terms, Paul argues that we could only know the unearned freedom of the Gospel and the healing power of the Spirit because of Calvary. As mentioned several times, this is not a theological theory for Paul, but the experience of the Christian. We suggested four corollaries in chapter 1 that derive from Paul's theology of the Cross; (1) we must also be "on account of others"; (2) our personal and communal priorities must be reexamined in the light of the Cross; (3) the Cross makes the weak strong; (4) the Christian church must share in the sufferings of Christ.

There is still much scholarly debate among Scripture experts on the connection between Paul's theology of the death and resurrection of Christ and Christian baptism.[37] A helpful guideline in understanding Paul's thought is to remember that, in praxis, he assumes the possibility of integrated experience in which the Cross, justification, conversion, and initiation into the dying and rising of Jesus form part of the same continuing event in the lives of the Christian church and its members, no matter how flawed they may be. Even when he is faced with the distorted theology of the Galatian Christians (due to the influence of some Judaizers) Paul challenges them to recall what they have experienced: "Have you had such remarkable experiences all to no purpose if indeed they were to no purpose?" (Gal. 3:4). I suspect that if Paul were addressing us today, he would still be posing the same question.

The Easter Vigil continues to symbolize, for catechumens and initiated alike, the remarkable experiences that God has done for us. We now return to Paul's theology with the limited purpose of understanding and appropriating (literally, "making our own") those same experiences. For ultimately, God will not ask us what Paul said about the Cross, but rather, what was the meaning of the Cross for us, and what difference did it make in our lives? Did our Christian initiation make us see the future through God's eyes in such a way that we "walked" differently each day until God's future was upon us? In brief, Paul's insights should help us examine the continuing effects of that night of nights in our lives.

Brave New World

Although the now famous phrase "brave new world" was originally used in a quite different sense, it accurately captures the central result of Christ's dying and rising as experienced in Christian initiation. I would offer the following précis of this Pauline conviction: *to die and rise with Christ is, first of all, to be freed to choose, to love, and to participate in God's "new creation."*

What seems to have prompted the development of Paul's thinking about how God sets us free and makes us able to be like Christ was the practical situation he found in the Galatian, and later, in the Roman Christian communities. For some converts, the old ways died hard. Especially for Jewish-Christians there was always the temptation to "earn" God's favor by observance of the law and its prescriptions, such as circumcision. Paul, in practical fashion, first argues from the experience of the Spirit received by the Galatian Christians: "Is it because you observe the law or because you have faith in what you heard that God lavishes the Spirit on you and works wonders in your midst?'' (Gal. 3:5).[38] Paul's question begins with an experience that the Galatians cannot ignore, and yet do not fully understand—God's justification. The Galatians' response in faith to the Word of God is not impugned by Paul but restored to its proper context—God's unearned, enabling, and liberating gift of love.

Because of Christ's self-gift on the Cross, we are liberated to choose God as Father. Faith sums up that radical choice. Paul cannot, in fact, use the term "faith" without inevitably speaking of its practical consequences—we are sons and daughters because of the work of the Spirit: "The proof that you are sons is the fact that God has sent forth into your hearts—the Spirit of his Son which cries out 'Abba' ('Father'). You are no longer a slave but a son!'' (Gal. 4:6–7).[39] Paul's readers, of course, were more sensitive to the difference between a slave and a free person than we might be, for their world was divided among the two groups. But we, the people of the twentieth century, also know the various and sometimes subtle forms of servitude that we have become accustomed to: a certain standard of living, assumptions about or "rights" to be free from the traumatic experiences such as war and famine that are a part of other nations' normal experience.

Freedom for Paul, however, is more than a metaphor. It is the astonishing experience of new possibilities and a new world never known before. This grateful astonishment accounts for Paul's sharp attack on those who would reduce Christianity to another form of religious and social control or a self-justifying "law and order" mentality. God's love, concretized in Christ's self-gift, is the only foundation on which the Christian can respond: "In Christ Jesus neither circumcision nor the lack of it counts for anything; only faith, which expresses itself through love" (Gal. 5:6).

Some years later, when Paul pens his letter to the Romans, his thinking on the problem of how Christians continue to misconstrue God's gift of salvation has considerably deepened. Especially in chapters 5 and 6 of his letter to the Romans, Paul succinctly and powerfully argues about the core of the Christian experience—"the gift is not like the offense" (Rom. 5:15). Our discussion in chapter 1, of the Cross and justification, allows us to concentrate here on the unifying symbol of these complex experiences: baptism as dying and rising with Christ.[40] But more important for the Christian is the realization that he or she can also isolate initiation from its wider context and implications and thus reduce this event to a contemporary form of magic or to a baptismal certificate.

The best place to situate our discussion of baptism in Paul's thought is in his startling statement on the effect of Christ's death: "For our sakes God made him who did not know sin, to be sin *so that in him we might become the very holiness of God*" (2 Cor. 5:21). The translator has rendered the Greek text's "justification of God" (*dikaiousnē tou theou*) as "the very holiness of God," which is, in fact, a very accurate equivalent. Paul has just been discussing, in the same chapter, the experienced results of how Christ has reconciled us, and proposes the insightful symbol that sums up these results: "This means that if anyone is in Christ, he is a new creation" (2 Cor. 5:17).[41] As always, Paul, as a good teacher, brings his readers back to the ultimate test of his teaching—their Christian experience. Both metaphors, "new creation" and "the very holiness of God," capture the effects of Christ's dying for us[42] as symbolized in the process of initiation.

In order to understand the pastoral problem that forms the background of Paul's thought, it is important to remember that Paul's readers most probably did not go through a lengthy catechumenal or candidacy process. The majority of these Christians had heard an initial proclamation of a suffering and risen Lord, and welcomed his gift of salvation in baptism.[43] Much of Paul's writing is concerned with the continuing education of good-willed but maturing Christians who have not completely understood the implications of what they have begun to experience as Christians.[44] In a real sense, our contemporary pastoral situation is not altogether different. Although we have Christians who may have received religious education even into their college years, this does not mean that they have examined their experience of Christ's dying and rising for them in their own existential situation. The result may be a Christian with a dichotomized religious identity: a good person with a baptismal certificate, some theological information, and with some religious experience. In other words, none of these autobiographical elements are, as yet, satisfactorily integrated into a Christian awareness of what God is doing in that person's life and the reason for it.

In chapter 5 of his letter to the Romans, Paul reviews the long history of how radical sin reigned and of the consequent human impotency to live out the implications of God's loving creation of humankind as "good" (Gen. 1:31). In a profound sense, Paul's statement, "but the gift is not like the offense," is a refrain that can resonate in the experience of the practicing or nonpracticing Christian if they will only take the time to reflect. The catechumenal process we have been describing in this book is the initial awareness and celebration of the truth of Paul's statement.

Caught Unawares?

When Paul gently probes the memory of Roman Christians with the question, "Are you not aware that . . . ?" (Rom. 6:3), he is drawing their attention to the "tradition" that has already been "handed over" to that community.[45] Nineteen hundred years later, it is equally important for us to answer that same question from the perspective of a dynamic understanding of "tradition." For some people, "tradition" is synonymous with "that's what I was taught" or "that's the way we've always done it." In other words, tradition is understood as a static body of information or practices that reduces its receivers to being custodians of a museum which preserves records or artifacts.

With the Christian community, tradition, or what is handed over to succeeding generations of believing communities, should not be separated from the Word of God. Like that Word, healthy Christian tradition is dynamic, dialogical, and dialectical. More simply expressed, both the Word of God and the Christian tradition that bears faithful and accurate witness to the effort of the Church to live by that Word, prophetically remind us of the presence of God in our midst. That presence does not exist in a vacuum, but is contextualized in particular times and places. The contemporary Church in New York or São Paulo shares some of the problems of Christian living and mission that Paul discussed long ago. But God's presence must enable us to deal as well with the unique challenge of living as Christians in this century.

"Are you not aware . . . ?" then, reminds us that we have been given much more than creedal statements and theological information. We have received the rich and continuing experience of God in the midst of other generations of Christians as well as our own complex religious experience. We have inherited the praxis as well as the theories and doctrines of Christianity. Tradition, like the Word of God, when handed on with fidelity, is a powerful witness to the mystery of God's saving presence among us. Such an understanding of tradition does not permit us simply to repeat what was said or done, but rather, helps us to "walk" the Christian way with a sense of continuity and creativity.

The Pauline Preposition

This understanding of tradition bears directly on the sixth chapter of Paul's letter to the Romans. This chapter contains a succinct but penetrating description of baptism, framed on either side by a discussion of the larger context of God's unearned gift of salvation.[46] Paul is not describing rituals of baptism.[47] As he weaves together the related themes of God's justification, its roots in the death of Jesus for us, and its sacramental celebration in initiation, Paul refers to his own and other Christians' experience of these realities as well as to the theology that it implies. "Are you not aware?" is not a rhetorical question, but rather, a direct question that elicits a witness to the living tradition which forms a part of the experience of all Christians.

If we, catechumen or baptized, are to make our own the power and meaning of baptism in water and anointing with chrism, we must come prepared with our reflected experience to these lines of Paul: "Are you not aware that we who were baptized into Christ Jesus were baptized into his death? Through baptism into his death we were buried with him, so that, just as Christ was raised from the dead by the glory of the Father, we too might live a new life. If we have been united with him through likeness to his death, so shall we be through a like resurrection" (Rom. 6:3–5).

Paul explains how we bridge the distance between Paul's Cross and ourselves through the initiation event in several striking ways.

First, the Christian has the same experience as the crucified Lord.
The operative words in Rom. 6:3 are the phrases "into," "into his
death," and "with him." Although commentators on these lines
may nuance their position, there is an impressive consensus that
Paul is attempting to describe how identical are Christ's and the
Christian's experience of the pivotal event of the Cross.[48] In order
to appreciate the significance of such an experience, the lengthy
discussion of the meaning of the Cross in chapter 1 should be
recalled.

Paul, in fact, does such a review in chapter 6 of Romans. As
G. Bornkamm has convincingly shown, if lines 5–7 and 8–10 of
chapter 6 are placed in parallel columns, Paul's argument is clear—
"In the baptismal event, the Christ-event is present."[49] When Paul
then asks, "Are you not aware . . . ?" the searching question brings
us back to the column of our baptismal experience and how the
Cross has shaped the contours of that experience. Just as the whole
catechumenal process prepares a person to see their profound need
and God's response in the life and death of Jesus, so the moment
of baptism effectively symbolizes the liberating result of that life
and death.[50]

But the baptized person will spend a lifetime "unpacking" the
continuing consequences of that experience. Paul gives us an example of how this is done. He urges the baptized, as those "who
have come back from the dead to life" (Rom. 6:13), to live accordingly and makes a telling comparison between their conduct as
pagans and their current situation (Rom. 6:15–23). Another way in
which we accept the consequences of our baptism is to survey the
inner landscape of our feelings. Long after our ways of thinking
and acting externally have been influenced by our initiation commitment, our feelings remain "mission territory." Our feelings can
have a life of their own, outside the control or survey of our minds,
if they remain an unexamined part of our lives. Feelings of deep
anger or resentment, nagging jealousy or boredom, for example,
may go unattended for years and surface only occasionally in some
external explosion. But Paul's conviction is that the mystery of
Christ's self-gift is so far-reaching that there is no corner of our
being that cannot be radically renewed.

Second, the experience of future resurrection begins with the current experience of new life. Paul focuses on the radical change of direction in our lives that dying with Christ brings about, if we are willing to "walk in the newness of life" (Rom. 6:4), as the Greek text so beautifully reads. We have already examined the biblical metaphor "to walk" as a description of our intentions with their values and priorities. "Newness of life" is a more elaborated form of a favorite Pauline expression "new creation" (2 Cor. 5:17; Gal. 6:15).[51] The result of being Christian, in Paul's experience, is a totally different set of possibilities in our lives. To "walk in the newness of life" might be translated, then, by a sports metaphor; God has given us in Christ a new field on which to play out our destiny. This new playing situation provides us with possibilities that we could never have fashioned for ourselves.[52] To make sure that we do not miss the daring comparisons between Christ's passage from death to resurrection and our own experience, Paul connects them with the expression "so that, just as Christ . . . so too we" (Rom. 6:4).[53]

This identification of our experience with that of Christ in the initiation event is so crucial to Paul's thinking that he draws on another set of images that do not always translate well into English. Paul challenges us: "If we have been *united* with him through the *likeness* to his death, so shall we be through a like resurrection" (Rom. 6:5). The Greek term for "unite" connotes a biological image of fusing what was broken into wholeness.[54] The word "likeness" in English suggests a photo of someone, but in Greek it connotes whatever makes the other the way they really are.[55] Paul is obviously struggling with language to express a profound and continuing experience in which an intimate relationship between Christ and the Christian is forged.[56]

Third, in initiation the Christian steps into the future now. Once more Paul is using images to carry a surprising message. When he speaks of "our old self crucified" (Rom. 6:6), the apostle is pointing to the frontier that separates a world of slavery from one of freedom, a world of despair from one of hope. With Christ's death and resurrection, a new age has been ushered in where God's reasons and purposes for creation will be validated.[57] But the Christian community and all its members have a role to play in this ongoing struggle. Paul reminds the Christians at Rome of their initiation and its perduring results so that they will participate in the work of Christ. In effect, chapter 6 of the letter to the Romans is a brilliant summary of the choices that a Christian makes: the choice between experiencing what Christ did or not, the choice between the "dark side" and that of light, and, above all, the choice between time with no real future or time that will usher in God's future. Our sense of time is focused and renewed as Christians because Christ's meaning gives new purpose to our use of time.

Living Water

Symbols such as the Christian sacraments enable us to enter God's mystery and participate in it. To receive a sacrament, then, is to be caught up in the meaning and experience of a crucified and risen Christ present among us. On the Easter Vigil, the Church calls down the Spirit on the waters (*epiclesis*) that she will baptize her catechumens in and renew her baptized with—these waters are the symbolic means of participation in the paschal mystery.

In the three forms of blessing this water of initiation (RCIA, pars. 215, 389), the Church uses a mosaic of rich images to help us understand the waters that we will use. First, there is a review of the biblical images of water: the Spirit brooding over the primal waters of Creation, the liberating waters of the Red Sea through which the Jews passed to freedom, the waters of the Jordan that Jesus stood in, the mixed water and blood that flowed from Christ's side.[58] At the Easter Vigil, there is an additional powerful image of the paschal candle as the light of Christ thrust into the waters, enriching it with his transforming strength.

As the Spirit is pictured in the gospel accounts hovering over Jesus as he stood in the waters of the Jordan, so the Spirit is now called down on these waters: "We ask you, Father, with your Son to send the Holy Spirit upon the waters of this font. May all who are buried with Christ in the death of baptism rise also with him to newness of life" (RCIA, par 215).

Water is still a complex symbol in our civilization: floods that destroy can be preceded by spring rains that renew our world.

When the catechumen steps into the waters of initiation, the dying and rising with Christ that Paul so skillfully summarized is sacramentally participated in: this ongoing destruction and renewal is the condition of Christians who are not yet in the Kingdom of God. Paul had been baptized many years when he sketched the tension of dying and rising that he still experienced in a difficult period of his own life: ''We are afflicted in every way possible, but we are not crushed; full of doubts, we never despair. . . . Continually we carry about in our bodies the dying of Jesus'' (2 Cor. 4:8, 10). (We shall return to this experience in the next chapter.)

Paul, in fact, constantly moves from the sacramental dying and rising to its transposed form in our daily living. N. Baumert suggests that there are three stages for Paul in this process of appropriating the paschal mystery of the death and resurrection of Christ: the beginning that occurs in faith, initiation, and other sacramental action; its gradual unfolding in the Christian's life-long struggle to be on account of others; and the realization of this identification with a crucified and risen Lord at the moment of our death and in the end-time for all of creation.[59]

The catechumen in the waters of baptism is moving into this second stage of learning—the cost and joy of becoming like Christ within the complex landscape of his or her own life-stage experiences with their crises and challenges. The strength to live and die, then, as a disciple of Christ is rooted in this identification with the central experience of Christ himself. It was this strength that enabled Paul to deepen his commitment to Christ in the most difficult periods of his life and to say: ''we carry about in our bodies the dying of Jesus'' (2 Cor. 4:10).

The Ultimate Warranty

The experienced buyer knows the importance of a good warranty that ensures repair or replacement of a product for a certain period of time. Lifetime warranties are rather rare these days. As we watch the catechumen being baptized or consider our own baptismal recommitment, we might wonder how long will this commitment last? No one, of course, can foresee all the implications of the commitments that he or she makes, nor can anyone guarantee that we will always honor our commitments. Paul, for example, is showing the Corinthians some of the practical implications of their baptismal commitment. In the middle of these considerations, Paul serves notice that fornicators, idolaters, thieves, drunkards, misers, and so forth, will have no part in God's Kingdom. He then pointedly adds: "And such were some of you; but you have been washed, consecrated, justified in the name of our Lord Jesus Christ and in the Spirit of our God" (1 Cor. 6:11).[60] Paul mentions Jesus and the Spirit in the same breath.[61] And it is this combination that is the warranty for Christian commitment.

Many Christians who were baptized as infants recall their reception of the sacrament of confirmation as a child or a teenager. In the catechumenal process, however, there is the unified celebration of Christians' initiation (including baptism, confirmation, and eucharist).[62] The RCIA has restored these connections because it shows "the unity of the paschal mystery, the pouring out of the Holy Spirit, and the joint celebration of the sacraments by which the Son and the Holy Spirit come with the Father upon those who are baptized" (RCIA, par. 34). After the newly baptized have received the white garment and the lighted Easter candle with a call to persevere in commitment (RCIA, pars. 225–26), the celebrant reminds the neophytes that Pentecost is not over: "The promised strength of the Holy Spirit, which you are to receive, will make you more like Christ, and help you to be witnesses to his suffering, death, and resurrection" (RCIA, par. 229).[63]

The celebrant then imposes hands on the neophyte and calls down the Holy Spirit: "by the water and the Holy Spirit you freed your sons and daughters from sin and gave them new life. Send your Holy Spirit upon them to be their Helper and Guide" (RCIA, par. 230). He then anoints each Christian with the oil of chrism in the form of the cross and says: "Be sealed with the Holy Spirit, the gift of the Father" (RCIA, par. 231).

In our own time the question of the Spirit has reemerged in a number of forms. The rapid spread of the charismatic movement brought with it the recurring concerns about when the Spirit is given. In the catechetical movement, there has been the ongoing debate for three decades about the age at which the sacrament of confirmation should be given. Contemporary theology has once again begun to reconsider the role of the Spirit in its discussion of the Trinity, ecclesiology, sacrament, and eschatology. These efforts to retrieve the importance of the Spirit in the life of the Church are one of the most valuable contribution sof twentieth-century Christianity. The starting point, however, for such discussions must be that of the early Church—the experience of the Spirit. Paul's question to some self-styled disciples at Ephesus is still pertinent: "Did you receive the Holy Spirit when you became believers?" (Acts 19:2).

For Paul, of course, belief and the Spirit are inseparable. Even in the Acts of the Apostles, with its apparently differing accounts of the reception of the Spirit among converts, there seems to be a consistent theology that connects the gift of faith and the Spirit. At Pentecost, there is no mention of baptism of the apostles, but they receive the Spirit (Acts 2:1–14). Shortly afterwards, there is the strange narration of the baptism of Simon and the Samaritans without the reception of the Holy Spirit (Acts 8:4–13). Only when Peter and John lay hands on them, do they receive the Spirit. The explanation for this situation is unsettling: "it (the Holy Spirit) had not as yet come down upon any of them since they hand *only been baptized* in the name of the Lord Jesus" (Acts 8:16, emphasis mine). In the story of the conversion of Cornelius, the Spirit is given before baptism (Acts 10:44–45). Peter uses this fact as an argument for baptizing these Gentiles (Acts 10:47). Finally, we have the case, already mentioned, of Paul's encounter with a group at Ephesus who had received the baptism of John the Baptizer. When Paul baptizes them in the name of the Lord Jesus and lays hands on them, "the Holy Spirit came down on them and they began to speak in tongues and to utter prophecies" (Acts 19:6).

Under this apparent confusion about the gift of the Spirit in the Acts of the Apostles, there seems to be a consistent theology that can be summarized in this way: *authentic conversion to gospel living and belief is inseparably linked to the gift of the Holy Spirit.* All of the accounts cited above from Acts are, in fact, a study in contrasts. Each story recounts how God's gratuitous gift of faith is received by people in various stages of conversion. James Dunn has aptly summarized this theological viewpoint in Acts: "It is not sufficiently realized that in NT times the possession of the Spirit was *the* hallmark of the Christian. . . . For Luke, as for Paul, the great difference between Christian and non-Christian is that only the former received the Spirit."[64]

One of the most succinct statements of this theology is found in Paul's second letter to the Corinthians: "God is the one who firmly establishes us along with you in Christ; it is he who anointed us and has sealed us, thereby depositing the first payment, the Spirit, in our hearts" (2 Cor. 1:21-22). The text is a mosaic of complex ideas, but a central idea—the Spirit as our warranty—emerges from these lines.[65] Paul sets the tone by using the phrase "us along with you in Christ." "In Christ," a much used Pauline phrase, refers to the unique relation of the baptized, communally and individually, with Christ.[66] The verb describing how God "firmly establishes" us in this relation is staged in a continuing present tense in Greek, in contrast to the completed action of the other verbs in the sentence, to underline this perduring faithfulness of God that continually accompanies us.[67]

Paul then employs three images to make us aware of the meaning of the whole conversion-initiation process. In the Old Testament, kings, prophets, and priests were anointed. Paul also seems to play off the meaning of Christ's name as "anointed" and the similar anointing of the Christian by the Spirit.[68] A second image, "sealed," was a familiar Jewish and Greek idea: it implies ownership.[69] As with the first image of "anointing," the "sealed" or marked Christian has the assurance of God's faithfulness. This is underlined by the context of this passage—the fulfillment of God's promises in Christ (2 Cor. 1:18-20).[70] The final image is an evocative one: God gave us a "first payment, the Spirit," or a pledge. Paul finds this image so apt that he uses it again in 2 Cor. 5:5. Everything changes with the gift of the Spirit in initiation because we have God's warranty—his new age and new creation has begun among us.[71]

Initiation, as celebrated and symbolized in water, the oil of chrism, and the laying on of hands is a paradigm for the continuing process of conversion. Whether we are speaking of the adult neophyte who has just been initiated, the teenager who is about to receive confirmation, or those long ago initiated, the pressing Pauline question remains the same: If God continues to strengthen us with that best of all warranties, the Spirit, are we responding to that call? In a world that does not seem to be a "new creation," it is all the more important that the Christian community remember one reason for which she baptizes and anoints: the paradoxical witness of a "new creation" enfleshed in imperfect Christians who have already begun to experience what they proclaim. This is the final parable about the Kingdom of God that the Church must continue to tell.

"Like a Dove"

Christians of the twentieth century have inherited a rich and sometimes bewildering tradition about the Holy Spirit.[72] As the systematic doctrine of the Trinity developed and the liturgical anointings of initiation were interpreted more extensively, the scriptural motif about Jesus and the Spirit was sometimes muted. In attempting to understand the role of the Holy Spirit in the process of initiation, there is always the danger that we will merely attach a theology to liturgical actions, and thus ignore the traditional guideline—the law of worship is the law of belief. In the pre- and postbaptismal anointings, in the epicleses ("calling down") over the baptismal water, and over the eucharistic gifts and the Christian community, we have primary references to the praxis of the Spirit among us.

We have already noted the importance of the Spirit in Paul's teaching. As always, Paul is not simply proposing a theory about the Spirit, but witnessing to the experiences of that Spirit in communities of his time. A second important source for understanding the Spirit in initiation is the account of the baptism of Jesus in the Jordan.[73] The four gospel accounts of the scene describe the Spirit descending "like a dove" and the voice from heaven speaking of Jesus as a "beloved Son" (Matt. 3:16–17; Mark 1:10–11; Luke 3:22; John 1:32,34).[74]

Without any attempt to psychologize the text, it can be plausibly argued that the event of his baptism represents a significant moment in the life of the historical Jesus.[75] Whatever theological interpretations serve as a background to the scene, this event coincides with the beginning of Jesus' public preaching and ministry and a certain awareness of the tasks that he was prepared to accomplish for the

Kingdom of God. Our purpose, then, is not to resolve the exegetical difficulties of the Jordan scene, but to focus on the meaning that is given to Jesus' ministry and the related role of the Spirit.

The Spirit, as already noted, is symbolized "like a dove."[76] Whatever the source of this arresting image, the idea of the Spirit in the Old Testament is a rich and varied one.[77] To help us uncover the role of the Spirit in the Jordan scene, we turn to the words spoken over Jesus: "You are my beloved Son. On you my favor rests" (Mark 1:11). Although Scripture scholars debate the possible Old Testament source of these words (for example, Isa. 42, Ps. 2:7), there does seem to be some messianic resonance to the text.[78] Jesus in the waters of the Jordan is seen as anointed for messianic service. Another New Testament source reflects on the scene and offers this insight: "God anointed him with the Holy Spirit and with power" (Acts 10:38).[79]

In other words, this is no idle pairing of the Spirit and Jesus at the Jordan. Isaiah provides powerful images that might well have inspired the early Christian understanding of the baptism of Jesus: "The spirit of the Lord God is upon me because the Lord has anointed me; he has sent me to bring glad tidings to the lowly, to heal the brokenhearted, to proclaim liberty to captives, and release to prisoners" (Isa. 61:1). Another Isaian image resonates even more closely with the symbol of the Spirit hovering over the baptized Jesus; "Here is my servant whom I uphold, my chosen one with whom I am pleased, upon whom I have put my spirit; he shall bring forth justice to the nations" (Isa. 42:1).

When the risen Jesus anticipates the events of Pentecost for the apostles, he promises them that they will be baptized with the Holy Spirit (Acts 1:5). There seems to be a conscious effort here to compare the apostles' anointing for mission with that of Jesus at the Jordan. As J. Dunn phrases it, "What Jordan was to Jesus, Pentecost was to the disciples. As Jesus entered the new age and covenant by being baptized in the Spirit at Jordan, so the disciples followed him in like manner at Pentecost."[80]

Interestingly enough, some early Syriac baptismal liturgies of anointing were modeled on the baptism of Jesus in the Jordan.[81] As Jesus is anointed with the Spirit, so the Christian is anointed with oil, which is "a dear friend of the Holy Spirit," as Ephrem says.[82]

As Jesus becomes King-messiah through that Spirit, so the candidate in this prebaptismal anointing is understood as entering into his Kingdom.[83]

The Jordan scene is still a normative model for the action of the Spirit in the initiation process of the Christian. The gift of the Spirit is inseparable from the coming reign of God and the service which it calls out of each Christian for the sake of that reign. The RCIA, in commenting on the interaction of the baptized and catechumens, suggests that Christians can "by their example lead catechumens to obey the Holy Spirit more generously" (par. 4). Later the RCIA provides the theological reference for this obedience. When confirmation is discussed within the process of initiation, the ritual notes "the close relationship between the mission of the Son and the pouring out of the Holy Spirit" (par. 34).

Viewed more closely, the role of the Holy Spirit as celebrated liturgically in the process of initiation, is a focused pastoral insight to be lived within the Christian community. The Holy Spirit is at the center of the conversion process and its continuing expression in the mission and ministry of the community. Like Jesus, we are anointed for service that images the Kingdom of God already begun in our midst. In the later theological development of the doctrine of the Trinity, this specific role of the Holy Spirit in the ongoing mission of the Church was sometimes obscured. Within the current ecclesial experience of the Spirit and its expression in liturgical celebrations, we can retrieve much more than theologies about the Spirit. The second eucharistic prayer for children summarizes this theology: "He (Jesus) promised to send the Holy Spirit to be with us always *so that we can live as your children*" (my emphasis).

The eucharist, another sacrament of initiation, also contains pleas for the Holy Spirit to come down not only over the bread and wine but also over the Christian community.[84] Historically, the ways in which the Holy Spirit has or has not been called down during the eucharist is usually revelatory of how the community thinks about Christ.[85] What is not noted enough is that the need to call down the Holy Spirit over the celebrating community also tells us a great deal about the problem of being church, the body of Christ: "Grant that we, who are nourished by his body and blood, may be filled with his Holy Spirit, and become one body, one spirit in Christ"

Eucharistic Prayer III). We will discuss this responsibility of being the body of Christ as part of our participation in the eucharist in the next chapter.

Some Conclusions

The theological and pastoral strength of the catechumenal process is that it effectively concretizes and clarifies the essential redemptive proclamation of the Church. Outside this process, crucial Pauline insights about our access to the Cross and the resurrection are often reduced to abstractions or pieties that the apostle himself would hardly recognize. In a profound way, the theology and the challenge of initiation is a continuing corrective to the ways in which we understand and live out our perceptions of what it means "to be in sin," "to be graced," "to be redeemed," "to witness," and "to welcome the Kingdom of God."

A case in point is the sacrament of confirmation. In pastoral praxis, confirmation is usually celebrated with young people who were baptized as infants. Although this sacrament has always been perceived with varying degrees of theological awareness as part of initiation, the implications of this connection have been more honored in theology than in praxis. Much catechetical discussion of the sacrament in the last three decades, I would suggest, has evolved in a vacuum, divorced from the larger praxis of the mission of the local church and from the praxis of other sacraments within that church. In a diocese, for example, where the praxis of the sacraments of confirmation and marriage have *implicitly contrary theologies*, what are the long-range results for the self-perception of that local church? In a parish, for example, where much is demanded for confirmation but little for the honest reception of the eucharist, what theology does this praxis implicitly teach Christians?

This is not a plea for pastoral rigorism but for the focused and yet compassionate theology of a Paul who can pointedly ask imperfect Churches, "Are you not aware . . . ?" at the same time that he reminds them—You are the Body of Christ. This former Pharisee who could defend the freedom of the Christian from the law against the Judaizers could also spell out the practical corollaries and demands of that freedom in the complicated context of the first-century Roman Empire.

Lent and Easter, therefore, are not static times of ritual celebration but a state of mind. During these seasons the whole Christian community stands before the mirror of God, Christ, and sees whether she has the same mind as that of Christ. Election of catechumens reflects the responsibility of the baptized. Creedal statements become thundering questions about a faith that must be still actively welcomed. The tradition of the Church with its long and mixed history of generations of other Christian communities who tried to live what they passed on to us is a challenge to our own praxis. Above all, dying and rising with Christ and the warranty of the Spirit take away our excuses for implementing the total Christian vision that the sacraments of initiation symbolize.

The church has always been aware that it is easier to confer sacraments than to live their meaning. When individual sacraments are understood and celebrated apart from the larger contexts of redemption, the mission of the Church, and the Kingdom of God, then their meaning can easily become unfocused for the whole Christian community as well as for the individual Christian. The test of the local Church's meaning is disclosed in the way that it celebrates the last of the sacraments of initiation, the eucharist, and then draws out its implications in a renewed sense of mission and ministry.

NOTES

1. *Protocatechesis*, 6: *Lectures on the Christian Sacraments*, Cross, ed., p. 4 (Greek text).
2. As J. Jungmann correctly notes, Ash Wednesday was a late development, perhaps not before the seventh century (*Pastoral Liturgy*, p. 246). The Lenten period only begins to take shape after the problems of the date of the Easter celebration have been solved; see J. W. Tryer, *Histroical Survey of Holy Week: Its Services and Ceremonial* (London: Oxford University, 1932); G. Kretschmar, "Christliches Passa im 2. Jahrhundert," *Recherches de Science Religieuse* 60(1972):287–323.
3. Canonical penance of the fourth century allowed the opportunity for forgiveness of sins once in a lifetime after baptism. In some Christian families of the time it was not uncommon to enroll the male children as catechumens but postpone their baptism so that they could have the advantages of being within the Church and still have the additional possibility of forgiveness after their "wild years" and their eventual adult baptism.

4. For typical citations and discussion from Ambrose and Augustine, see P. Brown, *Augustine of Hippo*, pp. 106–07; Kretschmar, "Die Geschichte des Taufgottesdienstes," 153–54.

5. The RCIA (par. 137) notes that these deliberations should take place before the rite of election.

6. If the celebrant was an active participant in the previous deliberations about the suitability of the candidates, the RCIA (par. 145) offers an alternative section that does not extensively question the godparents but rather summarizes the results of the previous inquiry.

7. *On Baptism*, IV, 21, 28. For a full but older English translation, see *The Nicene and Post-Nicene Fathers* (Grand Rapids: W. B. Erdmans, 1979), vol. IV (St. Augustine), p. 460.

8. My translation of his phrase in letter 16, 6(PL 54, col. 702): "*et exorcismis scrutandi, et jejunia sanctificandi, et frequentibus sunt praedicationibus imbuendi.*"

9. See Vogel, *Introduction aux Source*, pp. 269–70.

10. See Tyrer, *Historical Survey of Holy Week*, pp. 31–33. Vogel argues for an earlier prepaschal fast of three weeks that was eventually extended into a six week observance (*Introduction aux Sources*, pp. 271–73).

11. The familiar Roman Catholic praxis of confession owes much to a later penitential development called Irish tariff penance; see my *Real Presence*, pp. 156–79, and *A Roman Catholic Theology of Pastoral Care*, pp. 31–38; 44–47.

12. See Augustine's *Exposition on Romans*, 19(PL 35, col. 2102), E. Sauser's excellent discussion, "Baptismus—baptismus cottidianus—und Sündenvergebung in der Theologie des heiligen Augustinus," *Zeichen des Glaubens: Studien zu Taufe und Firmung*, H. Auf Der Maur and B. Kleinheyer, eds. (Zurich: Benziger, 1972), pp. 83–94.

13. My translation of Sermon 44, 1. For this and other Latin texts of Leo on the subject see the discussion of DeSoos, *Le Mystère Liturgique*, p. 89.

14. For the historical background, Stenzel, *Die Taufe*, pp. 154–57; for its later development, ibid., pp. 220–36.

15. In the fourth century church of Jerusalem, the pilgrim Egeria describes the intensive Lenten instruction in the "whole Bible" for three hours each day after the catechumens had been exorcized (46, 1 in Wilkinson, *Egeria's Travels*, p. 144). See also T. Maertens, "History and Function of the Three Great Pericopes: The Samaritan Woman, The Man Born Blind, The Raising of Lazarus," *Adult Baptism and the Catechumenate*, pp. 31–44.

16. R. Schnackenburg, "Revelation and Faith in John," *Present and Future. Modern Aspects of New Testament Theology* (Notre Dame: University of Notre Dame, 1966), pp. 122–42; here, pp. 131, 132.

17. Of particular interest here is the Johannine use of the Greek verbs "to see" as graduated expressions of faith; see R. Brown, *John*, pp. 501–03.

18. Ibid., pp. 178–80.

19. *Explanation of the Creed*, 9, as cited by Yarnold, *The Awe-Inspiring Rites*, p. 12, n. 47. For a similar treatment in Cyril of Jerusalem, see his *Procatechesis*, 12, *Lectures on the Christian Sacraments*, Cross, ed., pp. 7–8; 47–48.

20. For a discussion of this much controverted history, usually called the "arcanum disciplinum," and its relation to the catechumenate, see Kretschmar,

"Die Geschichte des Taufgottesdienstes," 156–59; Stenzel, *Die Taufe*, pp. 159–60.

21. *Sermons on the Sacraments*, 1; the text can be found in Yarnold, *The Awe-Inspiring Rites*, p. 99.

22. Kretschmar, "Die Geschichte des Taufgottesdienstes," pp. 157–58.

23. See J. D. G. Dunn, *Baptism in the Holy Spirit* (London: SCM, 1970), p. 150, n. 30.

24. *Confessions*, VIII, ii, 4. I use here the translation of J. G. Pilkington, *The Confessions of St. Augustine* (New York: Heritage, 1963), p. 125.

25. Ibid., pp. 125–26.

26. Ibid., p. 130.

27. For a thorough discussion of the theological and historical background of the debate between Augustine and the Donatists, see Brown, *Augustine of Hippo*, especially pp. 212–25.

28. For typical references and a summary of this evidence, see E. Dekkers, "'Symbolo baptizare'," *Fides Sacramenti*, pp. 107–12.

29. *The Sacraments*, II, 7, 20. I translate here from the critical text of B. Botte, *Des Sacraments, Des Mystères*, 2d ed. (Paris: Cerf, 1961), pp. 84, 86.

30. The baptism described here was celebrated in the baptistry, which afforded some privacy to the naked candidates. This privacy should not be confused, however, with the ecclesial and public nature of the celebration.

31. This paradigm of growth in faith obviously precedes the historical beginnings of the catechumenate in the second century, but is best exemplified in the catechumenal process once it is established. Stenzel (*Die Taufe*, pp. 79–98) confines his discussion to the historical question of whether there was a baptism "in the name of Jesus" or always a trinitarian form.

32. For the complementary nature of faith and sacrament, see K. Rahner, "Kleine theologische Reflexion über die gegenseitiger Beziehung von Glaube und Sakrament," *Fides Sacramenti*, pp. 245–52; especially p. 252.

33. PL 42, 179; the Latin text is cited by "Ostern in der Verkündigung des heiligen Augustinus," *Paschatis Sollemnia: Studien zu Osterfeier und Osterfrömmigkeit*, B. Fischer and J. Wagner, eds. (Basel: Herder, 1959), pp. 57–67; here, p. 59, n. 15.

34. See J. Quasten, "Die Ostervigil im Testamentum Domini," *Paschatis Sollemnia*, pp. 87–95; here, p. 87. see also A. Baumstark, *Nocturna Laus: Typen frühchristlicher Vigilienfeier und ihr Fortleben vor allem im römischen und monastischen Ritus* (Münster: Aschendorff, 1967), pp. 29–61.

35. *On Baptism*, 19, *Tertullian's Homily on Baptism*, translated and edited by E. Evans (London: SPCK, 1964), p. 41. See also, Tyrer, *Historical Survey of Holy Week*, pp. 19–30; A. Scheer, "Is the Easter Vigil a Rite of Passage?" *Liturgy and Human Passages: Concilium 112* (New York: Seabury, 1979), pp. 50–62, though I do not agree with some of his conclusions.

36. W. Marxsen has consistently warned against the danger of eisegesis, that is, reading into the texts of the New Testament a theology of baptism ("Erwägungen zur neutestamentlichen Begründung der Taufe," *Apophoreta: Festschrift für E. Haenchen* (Berlin: Töpelmann, 1964), pp. 169–77). His point is well-taken, though he seems to overextend his argument.

37. In addition to n. 36, see U. Schnelle for a summary of this debate in *Gerechtigkeit und Christusgegenwart: Vorpaulinische und paulinische Tauftheologie* (Göttingen: Vandenhoeck and Ruprecht, 1983), pp. 11–32. For a different

view, see R. Tannehill, *Dying and Rising with Christ: A Study in Pauline Theology* (Berlin: Töpelmann, 1967), pp. 1–43.

38. See Schnelle, *Gerechtigkeit*, pp. 62–63.

39. See especially Dunn, *Baptism in the Holy Spirit*, pp. 113–15, where he insists that the text is "another conversion-initiation context, in which the metaphors used build up to the culminating thought of the reception of the Spirit, and the correlative concepts of sonship and inheritance" (ibid., p. 115).

40. The exegetical debate about chapters 5 and 6 centers in part, around the relation of justification and baptism in Paul's thought. The debate, however, seems to be reaching some points of consensus. Tannehill, one of the more reasoned opponents of a baptismal theology as such in chapter 6 of Romans is correctly objecting to the isolation of this theology from the major themes of freedom from sin as the experienced proof of God's new reign (*Dying and Rising with Christ*, pp. 9–10). Schnelle, on the other hand, while insisting more on the baptismal motif, does contextualize it in these larger themes (*Gerechtigkeit*, pp. 86–87), as does H. Frankemölle, *Das Taufverständnis des Paulus: Taufe, Tod und Auferstehung nach Röm 6* (Stuttgart: Katholisches Bibelwerk, 1970), pp. 9–20.

41. I have dealt with this metaphor of "radical surprise" and its background in *Real Presence*, pp. 118–19; see also, J. Ysebaert, *Greek Baptismal Terminology: Its Origins and Early Development* (Nijmegen: Dekker and Van De Vegt, 1962), pp. 89–119.

42. The Greek text (*huper hēmōn*) is a technical and descriptive prepositional phrase that translates Christ's redemptive act. For its connection with the phrase "God made him . . . sin," see W. Popkes, *Christus Traditus: Eine Untersuchung zum Begriff der Dahingabe im Neuen Testament* (Zurich: Zwingli, 1967), pp. 236, 287.

43. See, in particular, Schnelle, *Gerechtigkeit*, pp. 48–49.

44. See G. Bornkamm's remarks in *Early Christian Experience* (New York: Harper & Row, 1969), p. 81.

45. This is much debated; see Tannehill, *Dying and Rising with Christ*, pp. 12–14; also, Schnelle, *Gerechtigkeit*, pp. 75–76.

46. There is an ongoing exegetical debate about the hermeneutical question of how the discussion on baptism (Rom. 6:3–6) relates to the rest of the chapter; for a summary of these positions, see Schnelle, *Gerechtigkeit*, pp. 76–77; Bornkamm, *Early Christian Experience*, p. 76; Dunn, *Baptism in the Holy Spirit*, pp. 139–41; Tannehill, *Dying and Rising with Christ*, pp. 7–14. It seems to me that the discussion is sometimes clouded by a distorted notion of sacrament, and by a lack of symbolic thinking that could connect justification, the Cross, and baptism.

47. Compare Dunn's understanding of "baptism in his death" as a metaphor derived from immersion baptism (*Baptism in Holy Spirit*, p. 141) with Ortkemper's questioning if there was immersion baptism in Paul's time (*Das Kreuz*, pp. 70–71).

48. See, for example, Dunn, *Baptism in the Holy Spirit*, p. 143; Tannehill, *Dying and Rising with Christ*, p. 22; Bornkamm, *Early Christian Experience*, p. 75; Schnelle, *Gerechtigkeit*, p. 76; Frankemölle, *Das Taufverständnis des Paulus*, pp. 99–107.

49. Bornkamm, *Early Christian Experience*, p. 75.

50. The "buried with him" image seems to refer to the ancient idea that burial is the entrance into the sphere of death, rather than a description of baptism; see Ortkemper, *Das Kreuz*, p. 73.

51. Ibid., p. 75, n. 464.

52. See ibid., n. 465; also, G. R. Beasley-Murray, *Baptism in the New Testament* (Grand Rapids: W. B. Eerdmans, 1962), pp. 212–13.

53. The Greek *hina hōsper . . . houtōs*. For a discussion of the significance, see Schnelle, *Gerechtigkeit*, pp. 76–77; also, Frankemölle, *Das Taufverständnis des Paulus*, pp. 53–60.

54. Dunn, *Baptism in the Holy Spirit*, p. 141.

55. See especially Bornkamm, *Early Christian Experience*, pp. 77–78.

56. The continuing aspect is brought out in the choice of tense for the verb in this sentence; see Ortkemper, *Das Kreuz*, p. 78, n. 489; also, Tannehill, *Dying and Rising with Christ*, p. 34.

57. See ibid., p. 30.

58. For Tertullian's early reference to the meaning of the blessing of the baptismal water, see Kretschmar, "Die Geschichte des Taufgottesdienstes," pp. 92–93.

59. See N. Baumert, *Täglich Sterben und Auferstehen: Der Literalsinn von 2 Kor 4,12–5,10* (Munich: Kösel, 1973), pp. 49–51; 51–58 for a useful set of charts that demonstrate these transpositions in Paul's writings.

60. See Schnelle, *Gerechtigkeit*, pp. 39–40; Halter, *Taufe und Ethos*, pp. 142–52; for the idea of the fullness of Christ's work expressed "in the name of," see Frankemölle, *Das Taufverständnis des Paulus*, pp. 45–46; L. Hartmann, "'Into the name of Jesus'," *New Testament Studies* 20(1974):432–40.

61. For the relation between Christ and the Spirit in Paul, see J. R. Villalón, *Sacrements dans l'Esprit: Existence Humaine et Théologie Sacramentelle* (Paris: Beauchesne, 1977), pp. 282–96. Villalón provides an accurate guide to the problem: "In the dynamic sense, each time that Paul speaks of the glorified Christ, he speaks of the pneumatic Christ, and each time he speaks of the spirit (pneuma), a christological sense must be understood" (ibid., p. 290); for the pre-Pauline tradition about Spirit, see Schnelle, *Gerechtigkeit*, pp. 123–24.

62. The historical separation of initiation into baptism and confirmation cannot be treated here. For a good discussion, see J. D. C. Fisher, *Christian Initiation: Baptism in the Medieval West* (London: SPCK, 1965); also, E. J. Lengeling, "Die Salbung der christlichen Initiation und die dreifache Aufgabe der Christen," *Zeichen des Glaubens*, H. Auf der Maur and B. Kleinhayer, eds. (Zurich: Benziger, 1972), pp. 429–53.

63. If the bishop is not present, then the presiding priest confirms (RCIA, par. 228) and concelebrants participate (RCIA, pars. 228, 230).

64. Dunn, *Baptism in the Holy Spirit*, pp. 66–67. I do not share, however, Dunn's prejudice against water baptism.

65. For an extended commentary, see Villalón, *Sacrements dans l'Esprit*, pp. 78–129; E. Dinkler, "Die Taufterminologie in 2 Kor. 1:21f.," *Neotestamentica et Patristica, Festschrift O. Cullmann* (Leiden: Brill, 1962), pp. 173–91.

66. So Tannehill, *Dying and Rising with Christ*, pp. 22–23; Halter, *Taufe und Ethos*, pp. 177–78; Villalón, *Sacrement dans l'Esprit*, pp. 91–96; *pace* Dunn, *Baptism in the Holy Spirit*, p. 132. For a comparison with the related phrase ("in Christ"), see Schnelle, *Gerechtigkeit*, pp. 106–22; especially, p. 121.

67. Villalón, *Sacrements dans l'Esprit*, pp. 84–90.

68. So, for example, Dunn, *Baptism in the Holy Spirit*, p. 133; Schnelle, *Gerechtigkeit*, p. 125.

69. See Ysebaert, *Greek Baptismal Terminology*, pp. 284–88.

70. See, for example, Beasley-Murray, *Baptism in the New Testament*, pp. 174–75; somewhat differently, Schnelle, *Gerechtigkeit*, p. 125.

71. For the connection of the Spirit and baptism, see Schnelle, *Gerechtigkeit*, pp. 123–35.

72. See Y. Congar, *The Spirit*, 3 volumes (New York: Seabury, 1983).

73. I have already discussed other aspects of this scene in *Real Presence*, pp. 120–22.

74. For a discussion of the variant readings of John 1:34, see R. Brown, *John*, I, p. 57.

75. See Dunn, *Jesus and the Spirit*, pp. 63–65. It should be noted, however, that the New Testament writers do not set up a comparison between the baptism of Jesus and Christian initiation as such; see also Beasley-Murray, *Baptism in the New Testament*, pp. 62–74.

76. For the problematic origins of this imagery, see F. Lentzen-Deis, *Die Taufe Jesu nach den Synoptikern* (Frankfurt-am-Main: J. Knecht, 1970), pp. 127–83; Fitzmyer, *Luke*, p. 483; Marshall, *Luke*, p. 153. The latter two scholars are less sanguine about such solutions.

77. See F. Baumgärtel et al., *The Theological Dictionary of the New Testament, Pneuma* 6:359–89; G. T. Montague, *The Holy Spirit: Growth of a Biblical Tradition* (New York: Paulist, 1976), pp. 3–115. For a perceptive treatment of the symbolic nature of the Holy Spirit, see E. Dobbin, "Towards a Theology of the Holy Spirit, II," *Heythrop Journal* 17(1976):129–49.

78. Lentzen-Deis' evaluation that there is no literary dependence on a specific Old Testament text seems to be a balanced assessment (*Die Taufe*, p. 193). See also, Marshall, *Luke*, pp. 154–57; Fitzmyer, *Luke*, p. 485; Brown, *John*, I, pp. 66–67.

79. This is Fitzmyer's suggestion, though he feels that "the idea of a messianic anointing is not clear in the baptism scene itself" (*Luke*, p. 482).

80. Dunn, *Baptism in the Holy Spirit*, p. 40; also, Montague, *The Holy Spirit*, p. 272.

81. The work of G. Winkler is particularly important here. For a summary of her work, see her article, "The Original Meaning of the Prebaptismal Anointing and Its Implications," *Worship* 52(1978):24–45.

82. Cited from one of Ephrem's hymns, ibid., 33.

83. Ibid., 36–37. Winkler points out that the radical change of meaning given to this anointing as an exorcistic ritual only comes at the end of the fourth century. The second anointing then becomes associated with the Holy Spirit. For some of the correlations in the praxis of the Western church, see her article, "Confirmation or Chrismation? A Study in Comparative Liturgy," *Worship* 58(1984):2–17.

84. For a full treatment, see J. H. McKenna, *Eucharist and the Holy Spirit: The Eucharist Epiclesis in the Twentieth Century (1900–1966)* (Great Wakering, England: Mayhew-McCrimmon, 1975).

85. N. S. Clark, "Spirit Christology in the Light of Eucharistic Theology," *Heythrop Journal* 23(1982):270–84.

connection with the catechumenal and initiation roots of penance. Easter Monday can bring with it the startling discovery of our flawed commitments. In the penitiential process that runs parallel to the catechumenal experience, we learn to "walk" again as Christian communities and individuals.

Easter Monday also suggests another question: Were we initiated into the Body of Christ for our private purposes? When the risen Lord appears to frightened and confused disciples, it is to reconcile them so that they might, in turn, minister to others. No one need ever be out of work as a disciple of the Gospel. The multiplicity of shared and individual ministries needed in each historical epoch are a form of continuing education in the postbaptismal period of our lives. One cannot remain a disciple without doing the work of the Master.

The whole process of initiation is, in fact, an accurate outline of what it means to believe and to symbolize that belief in the honest and fruitful celebration of eucharist, penance, and the ministries, ordained and nonordained, within the community. The initiation process is concerned with the ongoing formation of disciples. The resulting theology of discipleship can help us clarify the relation between faith and sacrament, the mission of the Church, and the Kingdom of God toward which the Easter Mondays of our lives are oriented.

The Daily Dying

Long after his conversion, Paul describes his current life as a Christian in a startling way: "Continually we carry about in our bodies the dying of Jesus, so that in our bodies the life of Jesus may also be revealed. While we are constantly being delivered up to death for Jesus' sake, so that the life of Jesus may be revealed in our mortal flesh" (2 Cor. 4:10–12). The point of comparison for Paul is the Cross as evidenced by the expression "being delivered" that he employs.[2] During the years since he was baptised into the death of Jesus, Paul has often sat at the table of the Lord. He had already explained the meaning of the eucharist to the Corinthians in his previous letter: "Every time, then, you eat this bread and drink this cup, you proclaim the death of the Lord until he comes!'' (1 Cor. 11:26).

In chapters 4 and 5 of his second letter of the Corinthians, Paul speaks of the difficulties of walking by faith, and yet affirms that his inner self is renewed daily (2 Cor. 4:16). As N. Baumert has noted, in commenting on this verse, ''Paul does not express here an abstract principle, but his own personal experience.''[3] This participation in the sufferings of Christ is not, however, restricted to the apostles. Paul has stated more than once that sharing in Christ's sufferings is the door to participation in his ressurection (Rom. 8:17; 2 Cor. 1:5–7; 1 Thess. 1:6–7).[4] The obvious question is: How does the ordinary Christian have access to the Cross of Christ? And how did Paul learn to incorporate so well the message and power of that Cross into his own life?

We appropriate the important meanings in our life through symbolic action. Unlike signs that only point the way, symbols challenge the limited meanings that we give our lives and they afford us a bridge to the realities they proclaim. Sacraments, as symbolic action, are not *like* something else, not *similar* to events in the life and death of Jesus. Like the Word of God, sacraments are the presence of Christ among us. Both initiation and eucharist are sacraments that implicate us in the death and resurrection of Christ. As Paul explains so well in chapters 10 and 11 of 1 Corinthians, we must make the meaning of Christ's death and resurrection our own. When we honestly participate in these sacraments, we begin the life-long process of adopting Christ's values, views, and life-praxis in our own situation.

Until the moment of their initiation on Easter, catechumens had only assisted at the liturgy of the Word. On the night of their initiation, they participated in the eucharist for the first time. The explanation of the meaning of the eucharist given to contemporary neophytes in the RCIA is the same as that given to the newly baptized many centuries ago: ''With the whole community they take part in the action of the sacrifice . . . by receiving the body that was handed over and the blood that was shed, they confirm the gifts they have received and acquire the foretaste of eternal things'' (RCIA, par. 36).

At first glance, this description of the eucharist in the RCIA seems only to reinforce the question suggested by Paul's discussion of participation in the depth of the Lord: *How* do we participate? But symbolic action helps us to rephrase properly the question: *Why* do we participate? "Why" is a question of meaning and the heart of symbolic action. In both the Last Supper texts and in the explanation of the eucharist cited above, "the body that was handed over and the blood that was shed" does not so much tell us how Christ died as why he died. As I have explained elsewhere, these eucharistic words are martyr words that spell out the meaning of the Cross—Christ as someone on account of others.[5] To participate in the eucharist demands, then, that Christ's martyr words and actions become part of our own living and dying.

The pedagogical context of a mature neophyte receiving the eucharist as part of his or her initiation into the Body of Christ is quite different from that of young children receiving their first eucharist. The whole catechumenal process entails an active and committed response to God's initiative in our lives and to Christ's life and death as a summary of God's meaning for the renewal of his creation. The Cross, as we have seen, is the pivotal element in this response because it redefines—paradoxically—God's wisdom and our renewed living. The highly condensed symbolic actions of initiation and eucharist summarize the previous conversion experiences of the catechumen and open a new chapter in the formation of the neophyte.

In the long history of eucharistic praxis and theory, there has always been a tendency to reduce the complexity of this mystery by asking "how" rather than "why." The "how" is a legitimate, speculative concern about the manner and mode of Christ's presence in the eucharist. This concern becomes misguided when it does not lead to the scriptural concern about the eucharist—why we should continue to participate in the dying and rising with Christ until he comes again. Since my purpose here is not to present a theology of eucharist as such, but to situate eucharist within the continuing postbaptismal experience of all Christians, I can do no better than return to Luke's Emmaus scene as a model for recognizing the Easter Lord in the breaking of the bread.

Easter Bread

Even with the best of teachers, some students are slow to learn. The disciples' lack of comprehension, despite the patient teaching of Jesus, is a familiar theme that is presented by each of the gospel writers in his own way. The Emmaus scene, as we already noted in chapter 2, is Luke's paradigm for conversion. By accepting the risen Lord as someone who first had to suffer (Luke 24:26), their own faith and praxis are reshaped in unexpected ways. The Word of God provided the vantage point for this moment of insight in their lives. In narrating this scene, Luke offers his own community a lesson in faith and its expression. Luke's narration outlines the problems of the neophyte or of the Christian seeking a deeper commitment to Christ. As we shall see, it also provides the context for understanding the eucharist as a continuing sacrament of initiation for the rest of our lives.

If we are to appreciate fully the careful structure of the concluding meal scene in the Emmaus account of Luke, we must recall how many other such meals are also recounted in his gospel.[6] J-M. Guillaume, in particular, has pointed out the rich fabric from which this Lucan meal theme is constructed.[7] Levi's response to the call of Jesus to discipleship is to give him a great feast (Luke 5:29) that occasions the Pharisees' criticism of the Master's meal companions (also, Luke 15:2; 19:7ff.). More surprising is the number of times that Luke records Jesus eating with the Pharisees (Luke 7:36ff.; 11:37ff; 14:1ff.). Luke also notes the meal of Jesus with friends such as Martha and Mary (Luke 10:38ff.). Finally, the parables of Jesus also privilege the meal as the symbol of God's Kingdom (Luke 12:35–40; 14:7–24; 22:24–27).

The key to the continuity of these meals in Luke's gospel, with the Last Supper and the Emmaus meal, is best seen in the disturbing lines of a Lucan parable. The master of the house, Jesus says, does not recognize those standing at his door. They reply: " 'We ate and drank in your company.' But he will answer, 'I tell you, I do not know where you come from' " (Luke 13:26, 27). In other words, not everyone benefits from eating with Jesus. The reason is not hard to find: the feast or meal is a powerful biblical symbol of pardon and fellowship, of the promise of God's Kingdom and its universal invitation list (Luke 14:16–24).[8] It is not enough to eat with Jesus. We must be willing to accept the challenging meaning of such meals. Recognition at these meals is mutual: we begin to "know" Jesus as we accept his meanings. The continuity, then, in all the Lucan meal scenes is the radical meaning that Christ gives them: the offer of God's present pardon and future Kingdom must be freely welcomed.

In Luke's Last Supper scene, these redemptive meanings are transposed to a new key. The Passover context is emphasized with its overtones of covenant and God's final feast. In Luke's account, Jesus speaks of a new convenant (Luke 22:20) and will not eat such a meal again "until it is fulfilled in the Kingdom of God" (Luke 22:16). Lest his readers miss the self-gift of Jesus in the Last Supper text, Luke frames his account with Christ's reminder to his quarreling disciples: "Yet I am in your midst as the one who serves you" (Luke 22:27).[9] But the question remains: Will the disciple, like the Master, live these meanings? The only alternative is given at the end of the parable about the guests invited to the great banquet: "But I tell you that not one of those invited shall taste a morsel of my dinner" (Luke 14:24).

Against this background of the interconnecting meal themes in Luke's gospel, we can now examine the meal scene at Emmaus with greater perception. When the disciples arrive at the village, they insist that Jesus stay with them.[10] At table, Jesus' actions are described in the traditional language of the early church: he took bread, blessed and broke it, and gave it to them (Luke 24:30; see also Luke 9:16 and 22:19). As W. Bösen notes, these meal actions with their implicit or explicit connections with other Lucan meal scenes are as clear in their meaning as they can be: "Death has indeed interrupted the line, but has not let it be broken. Formerly, Jesus took leave of his own with a meal; now in a meal he presents himself to them to be recognized again as the Risen One."[11]

At the beginning of the Emmaus walk, the disciple did not recognize the Master (Luke 24:16). At table they do recognize him (Luke 24:31). *But Luke has carefully structured the sequence of events in the Emmaus story so that the recognition scene ties together all the meanings associated with Christ's table sharing.*

Recognition for these disciples will entail the commitment spelled out in Jesus' disclosure of the meaning of the Word of God to them, and the acceptance of Easter pardon and eschatological promise in the breaking of the bread. Bösen's evaluation of the scene can hardly be faulted: "What I see is an old and familiar picture: Jesus as host in their midst."[12]

In Luke's model, the post-Easter problem of ongoing conversion and appropriation of the death of Jesus are sketched in bold lines. As with Paul, these disciples learn the meaning of the Cross from a risen Lord. Both Word and meal are symbolic actions that invite and enable participation of all disciples. Recognition of the risen Lord cannot be separated from sharing in the radical meanings of his life, mission, and death. Until these would-be disciples can accept the meaning of Christ's death, they can not credibly proclaim his resurrection. In the concluding section of this story, the Eleven at Jerusalem greet the returning Emmaus disciples with a proclamation that all can now share: "The Lord has been raised! It is true!" (Luke 24:34).

Eucharist is the Emmaus experience, given to us who are, like our predecessors, "slow to believe" (Luke 24:25). Though we have walked this way many times, had the Word of God torn open for us, and eaten at his table, we still have much to learn. To begin with, our belief in the risen Lord is clarified and deepened by the way we share in his dying. "And if Christ has not been raised, our preaching is void of content and your faith is empty too" (1 Cor. 15:14). In the eucharist as in the Emmaus experience, the disciple continues to learn how to recognize that risen Lord through a reappropriation of the meaning of his death, symbol of his total self-gift for the sake of all.

But this reappropriation of the meaning of "receiving the body that was handed over and the blood that was shed" (RCIA, par. 36) is not a private enterprise. Paul proposes to the Christian community a test by which they can judge whether they are, in fact, entering into the meaning of eucharist: "Is not the cup of blessing that we bless a sharing in the blood of Christ? And is not the bread we break a sharing in the body of Christ? Because the loaf of bread is one, we, many though we are, are one body, for we all partake of the one loaf" (1 Cor. 10:17). The ultimate proof of the risen

Lord is, as in the post-Easter gospel accounts, the reconciliation and unity of dispersed sinners.[13]

The Easter Body of Christ

Paul can sometimes capture in one line the complexity of several related experiences. An excellent example is his summary of the Christian life: "You died to the law through the body of Christ that you might belong to that Other who was raised from the dead, so that you might bear fruit for God" (Rom. 7:4). In chapter 6 of Romans, Paul had outlined the practical effects of dying and rising with Christ in baptism. In the verse just cited, while the primary reference of "through the body of Christ" is to the crucified Lord, Paul's thought cannot be disassociated from the related idea of the community as the "Body of Christ."[14] The transforming power of Christ's death and resurrection, as experienced initiation and eucharist, has brought us into one community but a community that "might bear fruit for God."

Paul cannot conceive of a community of idle holiness. If God has been generous with his unearned gifts of redemption and new life, it is so that these may be shared with others. As we saw in chapter 1, Christian communities can forget whey they are together and must once again be reminded to "heed the Spirit's word to the churches" (Rev. 2:7). If the community is being shaped by God's values, which the Cross symbolizes so powerfully, then it will bear witness to the world in its time. Paul's question to the Corinthians—"Do you not see that your bodies are members of Christ?" (1 Cor. 6:15)—cannot be isolated in the realm of sexual conduct. For Paul the consequences of being "in Christ," "members of Christ," or the "Body of Christ" transform living on every level.

What the neophyte discovers, however, is that some Christians do not seem to have read recently the twelfth chapter of 1 Corinthians: "The body is one and has many members, but all the members, many though they are, are one body; and so it is with Christ. It was in one Spirit that all of us, whether Jew or Greek, slave or free, were baptized into one body. All of us have been given to drink of the one Spirit. . . . If one member suffers, all members suffer with it. . . . You, then, are the body of Christ. Every one of you is a member of it'' (1 Cor. 12:12–13, 26, 27).[15] Paul's statement is prompted by the attitude of some Christians at Corinth, an attitude that has never completely disappeared from the Christian communities. The Corinthians had confused membership with being a member of the Body of Christ. Membership in a group carries limited obligations and privileges. But to be a member of a living organism is to be totally identified with it.

If Paul's implicit line of argument were paraphrased, it might run like this: if redemption in Christ is all that we say it is, why is there so much division and self-interest among you? Why do you seem to lack a sense of mission? The answer is simple enough: each Christian defines *koinōnia* or ''participation'' in his or her own way.

Koinōnia, a crucial Pauline term, is a Greek word is difficult to translate accurately.[16] We have already cited a famous use of the word in the verses where Paul is drawing out the implications of the eucharist for being a church: ''The cup of blessing which we bless, is it not participation/sharing (*koinōnia*) in the blood of Christ? The bread which we break, is it not the participation/sharing (*koinōnia*) in the body of Christ?'' (1 Cor. 10:16). Paul concludes his argument (one bread shared/one Body of Christ), and then proceeds directly to examine another form of participation: sacrificial meals.[17] Whether the Jew or Gentile, all of Paul's readers should have known the implications of ''participation.''[18] But did they and do we?

Two important and complementary effects occur when there is ''participation'': a new relationship to be lived and new benefits to be enjoyed.[19] Paul, in a penetrating argument, draws on these commonly accepted ideas to demonstrate how sacrament, Church, and living as people of a new age coalesce into the Christian commitment. P. Minear sums up these Pauline connections in this way: ''In all, participation in the body was in fact a participation in Christ's death, participation that when genuine, transformed from within all human relationships. This transformation produced societal interdependence that was accorded an unquestioned reality. Those who belonged to Christ participated as one in this revolution.''[20]

But Paul's argument has two sides: either one participates with or against Christ—''You cannot partake of the table of the Lord and likewise the table of demons'' (1 Cor. 10:21). In other words, if we understand the radical and transforming possibilities of Christ's death and resurrection, we cannot toy with their consequences. The efficiency of Christ's self-gift and its validation in the resurrection has been proved not only in the transformed lives of individual Christians, but in the redemptive oneness of imperfect communities of Christians. *Participation, then, is the gift that makes us choose.* In all the subsequent Easter Mondays of our lives, we continue to ''pick up the tab'' on the Easter events that we first celebrated in the sacraments of initiation.

Moreover, Paul's convictions about ''participation'' challenge some cherished pastoral priorities and sacramental praxis. *First, the theology of the Cross is enfleshed in the Body of Christ, the Church.* Paul is not interested in purely speculative statements about the Cross, Sacrament, or Church. A new age has been given for a new kind of people. The proclamation of all that Christ has done for us is verified in the Body of Christ that ''bears fruit'' for the sake of the Kingdom. But if a Christian community is judged by the theology of the Cross, then ''participation'' will be the testing point. The consequences and benefits of the Cross constantly spill over into human living and dying, and realign the intentions and values of the Church. *Participation, then, is the way Christians live initiation.*

The local churches or dioceses of a country or a region, for example, may have to choose between preserving the institutional security of the Church and prophetically witnessing to the gospel values which the Cross sums up. Archbishop Romero of El Salvador, for example, was killed while celebrating the eucharist because he led the Christian community in recognizing the implications of the Cross for the social, political, and economic situation of his country. His participation in the Body of Christ, eucharist, was not dichotomized from the body of Christ, as the people of a new age. When radical evil threatened to crush all hope for such an age in his country, neither he nor the local Church could simply ignore the situation, and yet be true to the Cross.

If the catechumenal process is the model for the whole Church as it continues to walk in conversion, then social realities that threaten to obscure God's presence in his world must be challenged with the peaceful resistance of the Gospel. Where radical evil is less dramatic and obvious, the responsibility of the Church to scrutinize the "signs of the time" is all the more important. In an American society, for example, that is so oriented toward a respectable consumerism and affluence, the theology of the Cross can be rendered innocuous in more subtle ways that can deceive Christians into believing that they can have one foot in the old age and another in the new. A credit-card society, after all, can easily tolerate Christians who ritually celebrate and participate in the death of Christ as long as they do not take it too seriously.

A second implication of participation is the connection between sacrament and mission in the post-Easter community. Mission is a term derived from the Latin verb "to send." There are many dimensions to the New Testament concept of mission.[21] In general, however, mission is the meaning of the Cross taken seriously. A good example is Paul himself. His own conversion experience of the Cross, seen through the prism of the risen Lord made him discard his narrow notions of salvation and its recipients: "Does God belong to the Jews alone? Is he not also the God of the Gentiles? Yes, of the Gentiles too" (Rom. 3:29–30).[22]

All humankind had shared in the impossible situation of being unable to welcome God's love on its own initiative. With the Cross the common problem of salvation became the potentially shared solution of salvation in Christ. In typically broad strokes, Paul sketches the cosmic sweep of God's salvation and its result: "Now all is new! All this has been done by God, who has reconciled us to himself through Christ and has given us the ministry of reconciliation" (2 Cor. 5:17b–18). Although Paul is speaking here about his own ministry, he expects all Christians to share in the work of the Gospel—the proclamation of this very news of reconciliation. Participation and proclamation go together. We cannot come away from participation in the eucharist without asking ourselves how this presence and its meaning is to be shared. "Everytime you eat this bread and drink this cup, you proclaim the death of the Lord until he comes" (1 Cor. 11:26).

But what happens to our Christian community if we give sacraments to our neophytes and long-initiated Christians but no accompanying sense of mission? Christ did not redeem us, after all, so that we might rest secure in Christian enclaves or ghettos. Paul's understanding of the sacraments of initiation as dying and rising with Christ is of one piece with the resulting reconciliation and mission of disciple communities of Christians. But one wonders if there is not a tendency for our Christian communities to become "service" churches that unwittingly encourage privatized notions of reconciliation and, therefore, of mission. In other words, is our sacramental participation and proclamation of dying and rising with Christ restricted to an "in-house" celebration that does not require us to look past our own needs to the fields ripe for the harvest?

Ministering Communities?

There would obviously have been no post-Easter mission of the apostles, if they had not first been reconciled by the risen Lord. After all, these are the disciples whose conduct during the arrest of Jesus is summed up in a single terse line of Mark: "All deserted him and fled" (Mark 14:50). In more positive terms, post-Easter reconciliation prepares those who are sent and thus enables them to be fully a Church. *Conversely, how we celebrate and think about reconciliation and penance usually reflects, for better or worse, our praxis and theology of initiation.* These statements are still not altogether self-evident in the post–Vatican II church.

In the new ritual of penance that was introduced in the post–Vatican II era, there was a notable effort to underline certain aspects of the sacrament that had been obscured in previous centuries. First, there was the emphasis on penance as reconciliation with the Church that is holy but always in need of purification: "Thus the people of God becomes in the world a sign of conversion to God. All this the Church expresses in its life and celebrates in the liturgy when the faithful confess that they are sinners and ask pardon of God and of their brothers and sisters."[23]

A second theological retrieval is the related issue of social injustice and our response to it: just as people join together to commit injustice, "they should help one another in doing penance."[24] The corollary is equally important: freedom from sin allows us to work with all people of good will for justice and peace in the world.[25]

In the decade since the implementation of the new rituals of penance, bishops and priests around the world have expressed concern about the dwindling number of Christians receiving the sacrament in any of the forms of celebration provided by the Church. These concerns prompted the theme of the 1983 international Synod of Roman Catholic Bishops, "Reconciliation and Penance in the Mission of the Church." (I will limit my remarks about the contemporary situation of the sacrament to the postcatechumenal concerns of this chapter.)

In a concise but challenging fashion, the preparatory outlines for this synod not only reassert the deep roots of radical sin in our contemporary world in its various forms of war, terrorism, oppression of the poor, and so forth, but stress the connection between personal sin and the larger societal contexts of sin: "It must, however, be asserted that the unjust structures are the fruit of personal sin in such a way that at the same time they offer to the person further invitation to sin. . . . The division which affects the world expresses in this way . . . that interior division which sin introduces into man, rendering him an alienated being."[26]

The contemporary Church can take a lesson from the earlier experience of Christians. After an initially successful catechumenal process of initiation and canonical penance (which provided a once-in-a-lifetime opportunity for reconciliation and penance after initiation), both sacraments lost much of their pastoral effectiveness in renewing the sense of mission in the Church, as even a cursory reading of the sermons of bishops like Augustine (fifth century) and Cesar of Arles (sixth century) will bear out.

When the larger purposes of being Christian are lost, the mission to the world and prophetic witness against radical evil—there is always a danger that penance and reconciliation will be reduced to the private consolation of Christians. When the ways in which we call our young people, for example, to deepened initiation commitment in confirmation and marriage are no longer geared to the wider mission of the Church, then how can the sacrament of penance teach them their need for healing on the many levels of their lives?

The best example of the connection that the early church made between sin and Christian mission in and to the world is excommunication from the eucharist.[27] Eucharist, as we have seen, is an initiation sacrament in the catechumenal process. Because eucharist, as Paul taught, is the symbol of the unity of the Church, certain divisive sins cut off the sinner from sharing in the Body of Christ (Church and eucharist). Thus, when a Christian's life-style and value-system seriously and consistently contradicted the meaning of the Body of Christ, the Church excommunicated (literally, cut off from that which is shared) this Christian by withdrawing the symbol of Christ's presence in the community—the eucharist.

The Church offered to such Christians the unique possibility of reconciliation in canonical penance to enable them to take part in being the Body of Christ in this world, and thus, receive the eucharist once more with its full Pauline meaning. *In effect, the Church in its penance invited Christians to appropriate the meaning of initiation and eucharist.*

The current malaise in the praxis of the sacrament of penance and reconciliation may betray a larger pastoral and theological problem about the popular conception of the Church that perdures more than two decades after Vatican II. If the metaphors that describe the Church as "Body of Christ" and "people of God" are perceived in static or purely institutional terms, then on a praxis level, the sacrament of penance is limited to the sphere of personal sin. If the credible proclamation of the Gospel is not regarded as the shared task of all Christians, then the theology of the early Church, as seen in a canonical penance rooted in initiation practice, has been adulterated. If the political, social, and economic results of radical sin need not concern individual Christians or their communities, then how does "the people of God become in the world a sign of conversion to God"?

H. Rikhof, in summarizing his inquiry into the way in which we describe the Church, notes: "It does not make sense to talk about a relationship in which a group or community . . . is involved without expressing it, and certainly not if the communal relationship to God is a constitutive element. *This means that the way the faithful as a community express the relationship becomes relevant to ecclesiology.*"[30] If a privatized notion of sin becomes the prevalent, or even principal, understanding of Christians, then their conception of what they are redeemed from as Christians, and what they are called to as Church will be an impoverished one. Moreover, this narrow conception of sin will have practical effects on the life of the Christian community.

The catechumenal process of initiation balances very carefully the complementary aspects of personal conversion and ecclesial accountability. More concretely, initiation is not some spiritual form of personal credit-card that carries certain privileges and obligations within a large and anonymous agency. Further, the sacrament of penance must be understood within the overall model of initiation into the Church.[31] The synodal outlines, already cited, reflect this principle: "In reality Christian penance is an essentially personal act, but it implies a relationship to sacramental reconciliation and entails consequences in the social field."[32] Reconciliation, therefore, is the continuing response of the initiated to witness to the world the need for and the results of a reconciled life. When reconciliation is celebrated in this way, the Christian community is expressing what Church has essentially meant to Paul of Tarsus, Augustine of Hippo, and Thomas Merton: a ministry of reconciliation that the world cannot afford to ignore (2 Cor. 5:14–21).

Some Conclusions for a New Beginning

In a well-known scene of E. Waugh's *Brideshead Revisited*, Father Mowbray, an experienced and perceptive Jesuit, is recounting the problems that he had encountered in giving Rex, a worldly and scheming pragmatist, religious instructions: "Lady Marchmain, he doesn't correspond to any degree of paganism known to the missionaries. . . . He was exceptionally docile, said he accepted everything I told him, remembered bits of it, asked no questions. I wasn't happy about him. He seemed to have no sense of reality." Waugh has another character comment on Rex's "conversion": "In her long history the Church must have had some pretty queer converts. I don't suppose all Clovis's army were exactly Catholic-minded. *One more won't hurt.*"[33]

The catechumenate began to lose its pastoral effectiveness in the fourth century when there was an influx of candidates whose motives for wishing to become Christian were sometimes dubious.

Although the Church in the first three centuries had had her share of imperfect or weak Christians, the public persecutions and social privations of being Christian demanded some form of communal and personal commitment even from these Christians. Waugh's comment about the poorly motivated convert (or Christian), however, is thoroughly disproved by the pastoral aftermath of the fourth-century mass of conversions. Although the catechumenate continued well past the time of Augustine in the fifth century to be the normal process of Christian formation, the masses of converts could not always be dealt with adequately. In the very sermons where Augustine expounds most brilliantly the Pauline teaching on the Body of Christ, one finds his pastoral laments about his own experience with a Christian paganism unknown to missionaries.

As I continue to have contact with various catechumenal programs in the United States, I feel a growing concern about the praxis theology that I see emerging in certain local churches.[34] In some cases, the RCIA has been treated as another program to be implemented or as a more appealing way of "giving convert instructions." Even in the best of situations, the local church does not always reassess her praxis and realign her priorities in view of the RCIA. If there is one certain criterion for the overall pastoral and theological success of the catechumenate, it is the way in which the local Christian community begins to discern what is the operative definition of Church as actually lived and celebrated by her people. The honest celebration of the RCIA renews the Church as it forms catechumens in the gospel life. With this in mind, I would like to conclude this book with a series of statements that summarize the praxis theology of initiation in order to encourage the local church to deepen its self-awareness, sense of mission, and perspective on the Kingdom of God.

1. *The experience of the risen Lord constantly brings the local Church back to the Cross and its implications.* A process of conversion and initiation faithful to the tradition of the Church leads to a shared and radical experience of a crucified Lord. This experience continues to question deeply the ways in which we either shy away from or appropriate the meaning of the Cross. *There is no commitment in the Church that has not been shaped by the Cross and the resurrection.* But the temptation to false "wisdom" is

never absent from the Church this side of the Kingdom of God. Nor has the foolishness of the Cross become more respectable than in Paul's day. The praxis of initiation, therefore, entails an ongoing reassessment by Christian communities of the implications of the Cross for the life of the local church.

Liturgy remains the training ground for learning the meaning of the Cross in our lives. As a reminder, both catechumen and baptized are constantly invited to begin their communal worship with the sign of the cross. The Lord whom we encounter in liturgy is the same crucified and risen Lord whom Peter and Paul encountered in the Easter events of their lives. Our eucharistic participation accurately echoes the meaning of our dying and rising with Christ and delineates the current practical corrolaries for living that meaning. Could we conceive of a Christian community uninfluenced by the implications of the Cross effectively teaching candidates to die and rise with Christ?

2. *The Word of God is a prophetically clarifying and enabling force for ecclesial and sacramental renewal and the prelude to any widening sense of mission.* Selective hearing of the Word of God is another persistent temptation within the local church. We cannot afford to hear God's Word in the same fashion that we switch television channels until we find what we like. The Word of God defines the cost of being *communio*, that is, the gathering of God's people, and enables us to be strengthened as such a people. For it is not the sum total of personal commitments that constitute ecclesial commitment. Rather it is the Word of God that allows us to walk together, united by a shared vision of God's new creation.

The catechumenal model structures the experience of the Word of God in a realistic way. As in the Emmaus journey, both catechumens and baptized learn to "recognize" the Lord when they continue to learn the meaning of why Jesus had "to undergo all this so as to enter into his glory" Luke 24:26). Thus, the Word of God bridges Good Friday and Easter in the daily life of the Church and provides an indispensable test of ecclesial self-awareness.

But is there a credibility gap between the theory about the Word of God and the current experience of the Word of God? The actual liturgical celebration of the Word of God and preaching in many places are sources of boredom, if not scandal. Priests, for example, who have been given, with canonical faculties, the privilege and responsibility of addressing God's people must be willing to participate personally in the Emmaus experience rather than simply talk about it. Once more, Paul suggests the testing point to those who preach God's Word: "We at least are not like so many who trade on the word of God. We speak in Christ's name, pure in motivation, conscious of having been sent by God and of standing in his presence" (2 Cor. 2:17).[35] To those who teach the Word of God in various ways within the Christian community, the Pauline reminder is equally applicable.

3. *The initiation process reminds the local church that the teaching of Christian morality should not be separated from the calling out of Christian mission from the baptized.* When the shared responsibility of proclaiming the gospel message in a way appropriate to each Christian becomes a normal part of the ongoing renewal of the local church, then what is specific and distinct in Christian morality is sharply outlined. There are many humanists who would put Christians to shame by their sense of moral responsibility. But the specificity of Christian morality lies in its radical shaping by the theology of the Cross and in its ultimate purpose—the witness to the coming Kingdom of God. In other words, to be Christian is not simply to "walk" well but aimlessly; to be Christian is to "walk" toward the Kingdom of God, and in no other direction.

Mission, as proclaiming and living the gospel message, focuses the moral sense of the Christian community in demanding and realistic ways, for the purview of mission is as broad and deep as the radical evil which opposes the Gospel. Whether it is a question of sexual conduct, business or medical ethics, the nuclear arms race, or social justice, the Christian response is constantly formed by the awareness of God's "new creation" beginning among us. "To die and rise with Christ" still suggests contemporary implications that shatter the polite moralities of Christian stoics. The celebration of penance and reconciliation within the Christian community, then, must reflect a grateful awareness of the gift of God's Kingdom and a responsible decision to witness to its coming in a world that does not seem to need it.

4. *The RCIA is ultimately formation in a lively hope that is based on the presence of the risen Lord in the Church.* If the

Christian has grasped the meaning of initiation into Christ, then his or her way of perceiving time and space is radically transformed by Christian hope. In Paul's view, hope is the second vision of Christians that permits them to live deeply and to witness well to the Kingdom not yet fully realized among us: "Yes, we know that all creation groans, and is in agony even until now. Not only that, but we ourselves, although we have the Spirit as first fruits, groan inwardly while we await the redemption of our bodies. In hope we were saved. . . . And hoping for what we cannot see means awaiting it with patient endurance" (Rom. 8:22–25). The youth of our era can find it more difficult to live with realistic hope in the sort of world that we bequeathed them. But it is the hope enfleshed in Christian living that challenges young people to walk to Emmaus with us.

NOTES

1. *Letter to the Romans*, 3, in *The Epistles of St. Clement of Rome and St. Ignatius of Antioch*, translated by J. A. Kleist (Westminster, Md.: Newman, 1961), p. 81.
2. See, for example, Barrett's remarks on "being delivered" (*paradidometha*) in *2 Corinthians*, p. 140.
3. *Täglich Sterben und Auferstehen*, p. 116.
4. See Tannehill, *Dying and Rising with Christ*, p. 86.
5. See my discussion in *Real Presence*, pp. 133–55.
6. For the textual critique of the Emmaus scene, see Guillaume, *Luc Interprète*, pp. 93–100; F. Schneider and W. Stenger, "Beobachtungen zur Struktur der Emmaus perikope," *Biblische Zeitschrift* 16(1972):94–114; J. Wanke, " '. . . wie sie ihn beim Brotbrechen erkannten' Zur Auslegung der Emmauserzählung Lk 24,13–35, "*Biblische Zeitschrift* 18(1974):180–92.
7. Guillaume, *Luc Interprète*, pp. 140–59; also, W. Bösen, *Jesusmahl—Eucharistisches Mahl—Endzeitmahl: Ein Beitrag zur Theologie des Lukas* (Stuttgart: Katholisches Bibelwerk, 1980), pp. 81–91; note especially the various sources of Luke's meal scenes on p. 88, n. 27.
8. See ibid., pp. 91–93.
9. I have treated this context as a theology of servant at table in *Real Presence*, pp. 138–40.
10. A very rare but strong verb *parebiasanto* is employed; see Bösen, *Jesusmahl*, p. 117.
11. Ibid., p. 115.
12. Ibid., p. 116.
13. ". . . it is the word of reconciliation through the cross that calls for decision, and that the decision relates to the new eschatological age that originates with the resurrection and opens the way to eschatological existence," in Barrett, *2 Corinthians*, p. 184.

14. Käsemann (*Romans*, pp. 189–90) is therefore correct in his interpretation, but as P. Minear has pointed out, "In this passage Paul stresses the total dependence of the community on Christ's death and their total interdependence in this event" (*Images of the Church in the New Testament* (Philadelphia: Westminster, 1960), p. 176; also J. A. T. Robinson, *The Body: A Study in Pauline Theology* (London: SCM, 1952), p. 47.

15. Conzelmann, *I Corinthians*, pp. 211–12, sees this whole passage as influenced by the "Body of Christ" understood as Church.

16. For an excellent discussion of the current exegetical positions on *koinōnia*, see J. Hainz, *Koinonia: 'Kirche' als Gemeinschaft bei Paulus* (Regensburg: Pustet, 1982).

17. He uses the verb "to share" (*metexomen*), 1 Cor. 10:17, and then, the participial form of *koinōnia* in 1 Cor. 10:18.

18. See Bornkamm, *Early Christian Experience*, p. 127; also, Conzelmann, I Corinthians, pp. 172–73.

19. Although I do not agree with some of their systematic applications of *koinōnia* in 1 Cor. 10, see the discussions of S. Aalen, "Das Abendmahl als Opfermahl im Neuen Testament," *Novum Testamentum* 6(1963):128–52 and Barrett, *2 Corinthians*, pp. 231–38.

20. Minear, *Images of the Church*, p. 189.

21. See, for example, F. Hahn, *Mission in the New Testament* (London: SCM, 1965); D. Senior and C. Stuhlmueller, *The Biblical Foundations for Mission* (Maryknoll, N.Y.: Orbis, 1983).

22. See Hahn, *Mission in the New Testament*, pp. 103–04; Senior and Stuhlmueller, *Mission*, pp. 171–72. Käsemann notes how Paul's statement directly challenges the rabbinical axiom: "I am not called the God of idolaters, but the God of Israel," (*Romans*, pp. 103–04).

23. *Rite of Penance*, par.3, 4 in *The Rites of the Catholic Church* (New York: Pueblo, 1976), p. 343.

24. *Rite of Penance*, par. 5, *The Rites*, p. 344.

25. Ibid.

26. In preparation for this synod *lineamenta* or outlines were sent to participants to elicit comments; see "Reconciliation and Penance in the Mission of the Church," *Origins* 11(1982):567–80; here, 569.

27. For a general study, see K. Hein, *Eucharist and Excommunication: A Study in the Early Christian Doctrine and Discipline* (Bern: Lang, 1975).

28. As the conception "Church" changes (for example, compare the ecclesiologies of Cyprian and Augustine), the notion of eucharist and excommunication will be affected; see W. Gessel, *Eucharistische Gemeinschaft bei Augustinus* (Würzburg: Augustinus-Verlag, 1966), pp. 158–62; K. Rahner, *Theological Investigations: Penance in the Early Church*, vol. 15 (New York: Crossroads, 1982), pp. 61–62.

29. Canonical penance had become pastorally inviable by the sixth century for a number of reasons. It was gradually replaced by Irish tax penance; see Duffy, *Real Presence*, pp. 156–69.

30. H. Rikhof, *The Concept of Church: A Methodological Inquiry into the Use of Metaphors in Ecclesiology* (Shepherdstown, W. Va.: Patmos, 1981), p. 234 (my emphasis).

31. "Reconciliation and Penance," par. 32, 576.

32. Ibid., par. 21, 573.

33. E. Waugh, *Brideshead Revisited* (Boston: Little, Brown, 1945), p. 193 (my emphasis).

34. For a survey of the practical implementation of the RCIA in the United States, see J. De Bone et al., eds., *Status of Implementation of the RCIA in the US: Survey Taken Spring, 1981* (Washington, D.C.' FDLC, 1982).

35. The Greek text is stronger. Paul uses the verb *kapēleuein* (''to water down'' the Word of God); see Barrett's remarks, *2 Corinthians*, pp. 103–04.